Sunset

Microwave
Main Dishes

❋ • ❋ • ❋ • ❋ • ❋ • ❋ • ❋

BY THE EDITORS OF SUNSET BOOKS AND SUNSET MAGAZINE

SUNSET PUBLISHING CORPORATION ❋ MENLO PARK, CALIFORNIA

Savory Smoked Pork Chop Supper (recipe on page 72) features an apricot-sauced chop, tender summer squash, and moist bran muffins.

Research & Text
Joan Griffiths
Mary Jane Swanson

Coordinating Editor
Cornelia Fogle

Design
Joe di Chiarro

Illustrations
Lois Lovejoy

Photo Stylist
Susan Massey-Weil

Photographers
Tom Wyatt: 2, 7, 10, 15, 18, 23, 26, 31, 34, 39, 42, 47, 50, 55, 58, 66, 71, 74, 79, 82, 87, 90, 95; **Nikolay Zurek:** 63.

DELICIOUS MEALS IN MINUTES

Many busy cooks rely on their microwave oven for reheating leftovers, cooking prepared foods from the supermarket freezer or deli, or performing odd jobs that make meal preparation simpler and speedier. Yet it's just as easy to use your microwave for preparing meals from scratch using fresh ingredients.

In this book you'll find savory soups and casseroles for the family, entrées perfect for informal entertaining or elegant enough for special occasions, and easy dinners for one microwaved right on the plate. Because all the recipes have been adapted for the microwave, they're streamlined to save you time and effort.

Remember, too, that foods cooked in the microwave retain more nutrients and have better color, flavor, and texture than those cooked by conventional methods. Generally, the recipes are lower in fat, since you can get by with less butter or oil than you'd typically use. Microwave cooking also simplifies cleanup— most entrées are cooked and served in a single dish. Preparing meals in hot weather is a breeze, because you can cook without heating up the kitchen.

Preparation and cooking times accompany each recipe. We also provide a nutritional analysis (see page 8) prepared by Hill Nutrition Associates, Inc., of Florida.

We thank Rebecca LaBrum for her skillful and thorough editing of the text, and Viki Marugg for her creative contributions in developing the art. We also extend thanks to The Best of All Worlds, Cookin', Crate & Barrel, The Pottery Barn, and Sue Fisher King for sharing props used in our photographs.

Cover: Traditional taste in half the usual time—that's the reward our hearty Quick Paella (recipe on page 86) offers you. Chicken, shrimp, and sausage mingle with bell peppers and saffron-tinted rice in this classic one-dish meal. Design by Susan Bryant. Photography by Tom Wyatt. Photo styling by Susan Massey-Weil. Food styling by Mary Jane Swanson.

About the Recipes

All of the recipes in this book were tested and developed in the Sunset test kitchens.

Food and Entertaining Editor, *Sunset* Magazine
Jerry Anne Di Vecchio

Editor, Sunset Books: Elizabeth L. Hogan

Third printing October 1991

CONTENTS

Real Food from the Microwave

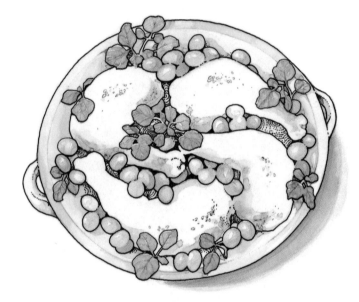

In today's fast-paced world, the question "What's for dinner?" is often met with a groan. Most of us just don't have the time to plan and prepare the well-balanced family meal that was so typical only a generation ago.

Given the constraints of hectic and often conflicting schedules, it's no surprise that over three-fourths of American households have invested in a microwave oven to make meal preparation simpler and speedier. Unfortunately, many of us use the microwave just to reheat the leftovers from Saturday's party or prepare some *haute cuisine* from the supermarket freezer case. But as this book will show you, you can produce real food from the microwave almost as easily.

Your favorite soups, stews, casseroles, meat dishes, and other main courses can be ready to serve in less (sometimes much less!) than half the time you'd need to cook them conventionally. Choose from entrées for one, microwaved right on a dinner plate, or casseroles for a family of six. You'll even find a number of decidedly elegant selections, perfect for special occasions or spur-of-the-moment entertaining.

MICROWAVE BENEFITS

Speeded-up cooking isn't the only advantage microwaving offers. Microwaved entrées—particularly those based on chicken, fish, or vegetables—retain more color, flavor, and texture. Retention of nutrients, especially the water-soluble vitamins B and C, is greater as well. There's another health benefit, too—microwaved dishes are often lower in fat than their conventionally cooked counterparts, since you can get by with less butter or oil than you'd typically use.

Because the oven cavity doesn't heat up, microwave cooking is a real boon to hot-weather cooks: your kitchen doesn't turn into a furnace, and no blast of hot air greets you when you open the door to check or remove food.

Best of all, perhaps, is the great reduction in cleanup. Since our main dishes are usually cooked and served in a single baking dish or casserole, you'll save yourself the chore of washing extra pots and pans.

HOW DOES THE MICROWAVE WORK?

If you're new to microwave cooking, take the time to learn how your oven works.

The heart of the microwave is the *magnetron tube,* which converts ordinary household electricity into high-frequency microwaves. When they reach the oven cavity, the microwaves are distributed by a metal-bladed *stirrer fan.* Depending upon the materials they contact, the waves act in different ways: they'll reflect from some substances, simply pass through others, and be absorbed by still others.

Because *metal reflects microwaves,* the basic wall material and stirrer fan are made of metal. *Glass, pottery, paper, and plastic allow microwaves to pass through,* so these are used for cooking containers and coverings. **Containers can pick up heat from the food itself, though—so if a dish has been in the oven for a fair amount of time, be sure to handle it with potholders.**

The water, fat, and sugar in foods absorb microwaves, which in turn cause the molecules in the food to vibrate rapidly. That leads to friction, heat, and—ultimately—cooking. Since microwaves generally penetrate to a depth of only ¾ to 1½ inches, the center of a large mass, such as a roast or a good-sized casserole, will be cooked not by microwave energy, but by the surrounding heat as it's conducted inward.

The air in the oven isn't affected by microwaves, so it usually stays cool. But be aware that quite a lot of steam can become trapped inside covered cooking containers. **To avoid steam burns, always be very careful when uncovering dishes; remove the lids so that any steam will escape away from you.**

HOW OVENS DIFFER—IT'S THE WATTAGE THAT COUNTS

You'll find a staggering array of microwave ovens on the market today. The portable countertop model is still the most popular, but demand is increasing for built-in types—installed over a range, beneath a cabinet, or as the top unit of a double wall oven.

A number of special features are available, too. Some ovens have carousels that rotate cooking dishes for you; others have probes, thermometerlike devices that detect the temperature of whatever you're heating. And some ovens can be programmed to defrost and cook foods ahead of time.

Whatever their design, all microwave ovens cook food in the same way. **The one important difference among ovens is the wattage (cooking power): the higher the wattage, the faster foods will cook.**

If you have a fairly new full-size oven, the wattage on full power or **HIGH (100%)** probably ranges from 600 to 700 watts. Older, small, or less expensive ovens, on the other hand, may have a full power of only 450 to 500 watts.

To find out the wattage of your oven, check the owner's manual. Or perform this simple test. Fill a 1-cup glass measure with room-temperature water (72°F). Place the cup on the oven floor. Microwave, uncovered, on **HIGH (100%)** until the water comes to a boil, noting the time required. If the oven is in the 600- to 700-watt range, the water will boil in 2½ to 3 minutes.

WHAT ABOUT ALL THOSE POWER LEVELS?

Any microwave offers you a choice of power levels, but the number of different levels provided varies with the oven. Some types have a range of 10 power settings, usually set up as a 10-button touch pad; number 1 equals 10% power, number 10 equals 100%. Ovens with five power levels are popular, too; the settings are typically labeled **LOW, MEDIUM-LOW, MEDIUM, MEDIUM-HIGH,** and **HIGH.** If you use an older or less expensive model, your choices may be more limited. The oven may have only full power (100%); only full power and half power (50%); or only full power and defrost (usually 30%, but some older ovens may have a defrost setting of 50% power).

THE MICROWAVE WE USED

To test all our microwave main-dish recipes, we used 600- to 700-watt ovens, both 10- and five-power-level models. These are the most popular ovens on the market as this book goes to print.

If you own an oven with less than 600 to 700 watts of cooking power, keep in mind that, at every step, the correct microwaving times for you will vary from those we give. Still, you should always start with the minimum time given, then cook foods longer, in 30-second to 1-minute increments, as needed.

In each recipe, you'll be instructed to cook at one or more of the following power levels:

HIGH (100%)
MEDIUM-HIGH (70–80%)
MEDIUM (50%)
MEDIUM–LOW (30%)
LOW (10–20%)

In the majority of cases, you'll be using just **HIGH (100%)** or **MEDIUM (50%),** but occasionally the other levels are specified. If your oven lacks the required setting, you'll probably need to adjust the cooking times.

WHAT AFFECTS COOKING TIME?

An oven's wattage and the power level used aren't the only variables that influence the time needed to microwave foods just right. Keep these three factors in mind as well:

■ *The quantity of food in the oven.* More food in the microwave means a longer cooking time. While a single boneless chicken breast half takes only 2½ minutes to cook, six halves may take up to 6 minutes. And a chicken breast that's cooked with vegetables or a sauce will take longer than one that's microwaved unadorned. If you vary the quantities in our recipes, remember that the timing will change.

■ *Initial temperature of foods.* Cold foods, taken straight from the refrigerator, require longer cooking than room-temperature foods.

■ *Density of foods.* The denser the food, the less easily microwaves can penetrate it. For this reason, a dense food such as a steak has a longer cooking time than an equivalent amount of a less dense food like a sole fillet.

TECHNIQUES FOR EVEN COOKING

Microwaves penetrate foods only to a limited distance, and some ovens tend to cook rather unevenly. For these reasons, you'll get better results with many recipes if you devote some extra attention to techniques for even cooking.

Begin by checking your oven's heating pattern. Cut a piece of smooth brown paper the size of the oven floor; wet the paper, place it in the oven, and microwave on **HIGH (100%)** for 1 minute. Note where the paper is still damp; in these areas, food will take longer to cook.

(Continued on page 8)

Deliciously rich Pea Pod & Shrimp Pasta (recipe on page 30) combines fresh linguine, Chinese pea pods, and succulent shrimp in a luxurious sauce of cream and Swiss cheese. To complete an elegant lunch or supper menu, add a salad, your favorite dinner rolls, and a chilled white wine.

To compensate for any tendency toward uneven cooking, be sure to arrange foods properly in the cooking dish, and to stir or rearrange the food or rotate the dish periodically during microwaving. You'll find instructions for these techniques in each recipe.

■ *Arranging foods correctly* is necessary for even microwaving. For example, when cooking chicken legs, always position them with the thickest part (the thighs) toward the outside of the dish, where foods cook more quickly. And when microwaving chopped vegetables or other small pieces of food, spread them out in an even layer before you start to cook—and again after stirring.

■ *Rearranging foods* partway through cooking may be necessary, too. Foods of even thickness, such as fish steaks, can simply be turned around to bring the uncooked parts to the outside. If the thickness varies (as for pork ribs, for instance), you'll need to move the pieces around more—bring those at the center of the dish to the edges, and vice versa.

■ *Stirring* is especially important for sauces, but it's also vital when you're "sautéing" foods. When microwaving mushrooms or onions, for example, you should stir them every few minutes to bring the cooked pieces to the center of the dish and push the uncooked ones to the outside.

■ *Rotating* a dish or casserole ensures that foods microwave equally on all sides; it also helps even out the effects of your oven's hot spots. Most recipes will tell you to give the dish a half-turn; that is,

rotate it so the portion closest to the back of the oven ends up nearest the front. (If your oven has a carousel, rotating may not be necessary.)

THE IMPORTANCE OF STANDING TIME

Foods keep cooking after you take them from any oven, but the extent of additional cooking is much greater for microwave than for conventional ovens. When a recipe gives a standing time, pay attention to it. Our Asparagus & Ham Strata (page 22), for example, must stand for 10 minutes to set up and finish cooking in the center. If you let it stand for 20 minutes, it will be overdone; if you don't let it stand at all, it will be undercooked when you serve it.

MICROWAVE-SAFE CONTAINERS & COVERS

Containers for microwave main dishes should be made of materials that allow microwave energy to pass through. **Your best choices are heatproof glassware and ceramics, and heatproof plastic (thermoplastic) designed for microwave cooking.** Besides bowls, baking dishes, and casseroles, you'll find glass measuring cups in a range of sizes very useful; they're particularly handy for making sauces and gravies.

CAUTION: Avoid metal containers and any dishes with metallic, especially gold or silver, trim (gold-rimmed china plates, for example). Metal reflects microwaves and may cause *arcing* in the oven (you'll see what looks like lightning or sparks). Arcing can eventually damage the magnetron tube.

Pottery, plastic, and china may or may not be appropriate for the microwave. In some cases, these materials have components that interfere with the transmission of microwaves, so check with the manufacturer to make sure your dishes are microwave-safe. If you're not certain, you can find out by performing this test. Fill a glass measure with 1 cup water, then place it in the microwave alongside the dish in question. Microwave on **HIGH (100%)** for 1 minute. Only the water should get hot; if the dish heats up too, don't use it in your oven.

Plastic foam plates and cups are suitable for heating food just until warm, but don't use them for actual cooking.

A WORD ABOUT OUR NUTRITIONAL DATA

For our recipes, we provide a nutritional analysis stating calorie count; grams of protein, carbohydrates, and total fat; and milligrams of cholesterol and sodium. Generally, the analysis applies to a single serving, based on the number of servings given for each recipe and the amount of each ingredient. If a range is given for the number of servings and/or the amount of an ingredient, the analysis is based on an average of the figures given.

The nutritional analysis does not include optional ingredients or those for which no specific amount is stated. If an ingredient is listed with a substitution, the information was calculated using the first choice.

Plastic bags can be used in the microwave if they're the heavy-duty type; avoid the thin plastic bags provided in the produce departments of most grocery stores. To close the bags, simply knot them at the top; or use a piece of string, a plastic holder, or a rubber band. *Don't use twist ties,* since they contain metal.

Paper plates, cups, napkins, and towels can be used in the microwave.

Plastic wrap and glass or ceramic lids are good container covers. These are the best choices when the recipe tells you to "cover and microwave." We recommend using the heavy-duty plastic wrap specifically designed for microwave use; lightweight, inexpensive wraps may split during cooking and melt into the food. *(Don't use plastic wrap to cover a hot microwave browning dish,* though; always use the dish lid.)

Wax paper is appropriate when you want to cover foods loosely.

Aluminum foil is a subject of some controversy among microwave manufacturers. Most makers agree that a limited amount may be used to shield parts of food that are likely to cook too fast—wingtips of poultry or tails of whole fish, for example—but others oppose using foil at any time. Check your owner's manual to see what's recommended for your particular oven. *We do not recommend using foil in our recipes.*

SPECIALTY EQUIPMENT

The *microwave browning dish* is one piece of specialty equipment we found very helpful for adding color and appealing browned flavor to some of our meat, fish, and poultry recipes, such as Steak with Mustard-Caper Sauce (page 36), Walla Walla Salmon (page 59), and the Quick Paella (page 86) pictured on the front cover.

To use a browning dish, preheat it in the microwave on **HIGH (100%)** for the time indicated in the recipe (usually 4½ minutes). Using potholders or oven mitts, carefully transfer the dish to a heatproof surface, keeping in mind that the bottom will be very hot. Then add oil or other fat (if directed) and the food to be seared. Browning dishes maintain their heat for just a few minutes, so the food you add will usually be darker on the side that's browned first.

Microwave-safe racks or meat racks are also referred to in this book. Such racks have a couple of uses. Set over a microwave-safe baking dish, they can, of course, be used as roasting racks for chicken, meats, or strips of bacon, allowing the fat to drain from the food into the dish below. And you can use a rack to elevate a baking dish or casserole; this helps distribute the oven's heat more evenly, since waves can now penetrate from underneath as well as from the sides. (Elevating the dish is particularly helpful when you're cooking a casserole that can't be stirred, such as lasagne.)

Other specialty equipment includes cupcakers, bacon trees, ring molds, thermometers, popcorn poppers, and plastic shelves that let you put more food in the oven at once. You may want to buy one or more of these items, but you won't need any of them to prepare the recipes in this book.

MOVING ON TO MICROWAVE CUISINE

You've read up on the basics of microwave techniques and reviewed some do's and don'ts. Now it's time to take the next step: move on to quicker, more healthful meals for your family, guests, or just you. A whole book full of great recipes is right in front of you!

Please all of the people all of the time with our Chunky Condiment Chili (recipe on page 13). Dotted with corn kernels and diced red pepper, the spicy chili gets dressed up at the table to suit each diner's taste. Provide as many toppings as you like; we show cheese, onions, yogurt, and tortilla chips.

Chilis, Soups & Stews

Homemade chili, hearty soups, filling stews—once upon a time, you had to wait through hours of simmering to enjoy these satisfying dishes. But the microwave oven has changed all that. Today, you can put these sturdy entrées together in less than half the traditional cooking time. In this chapter, we've included some perennial favorites—creamy corn chowder, robust cioppino, thick chili, even Moroccan couscous. Any of our recipes is a perfect choice for a homey meal that's sure to delight both family and guests.

BEEF & CHORIZO CHILI

Preparation time: 15 minutes
Microwaving time: 23 to 30 minutes
Standing time: 3 to 5 minutes

This rich, red chili freezes well for a second meal, but it's so good that you probably won't have any leftovers.

- 1½   pounds lean ground beef
- ½   pound chorizo sausage, casings removed, meat cut into ½-inch-thick slices
- 1   medium-size onion, thinly sliced
- 2   cloves garlic, minced or pressed
- 3   to 4 tablespoons chili powder
- 1   teaspoon *each* dry oregano leaves and ground cumin
- 1   can (14½ oz.) diced tomatoes in purée
- 1   can (about 1 lb.) kidney beans
- 1   can (8 oz.) tomato sauce
- 4   to 6 cups shredded iceberg lettuce or corn chips
     About ⅔ cup *each* shredded jack cheese and sharp Cheddar cheese

Crumble beef into a 3- to 4-quart microwave-safe casserole; add chorizo. Microwave, uncovered, on **HIGH (100%)** for 8 to 10 minutes or until beef is no longer pink, stirring every 3 minutes. Spoon off and discard all but 2 tablespoons of the drippings. Stir in onion, garlic, chili powder, oregano, and cumin. Microwave, uncovered, on **HIGH (100%)** for 3 to 5 minutes or until onion is soft, stirring after 2 minutes.

Stir in tomatoes, undrained beans, and tomato sauce. Cover and microwave on **HIGH (100%)** for 12 to 15 minutes or until chili is bubbly all over, stirring every 4 minutes. Let stand, covered, for 3 to 5 minutes.

Line individual bowls with lettuce and top with chili. Sprinkle with jack and Cheddar cheeses. Makes 4 to 6 servings.

Per serving: 677 calories, 46 g protein, 31 g carbohydrates, 42 g total fat, 139 mg cholesterol, 1,166 mg sodium

TURKEY & RED BEAN CHILI

Preparation time: 5 to 10 minutes
Microwaving time: 34 to 39 minutes
Standing time: 5 minutes

Here's a contemporary version of chili con carne that's a bit on the lighter side. Ground turkey and diced green chiles mingle with the traditional tomatoes and plenty of kidney beans.

- 1   tablespoon salad oil
- 1   pound ground turkey
- 1   medium-size onion, chopped
- 1   or 2 large cans (7 oz. *each*) diced green chiles
- 1   can (14½ oz.) regular-strength chicken broth
- 1   can (14½ oz.) tomatoes
- ½   teaspoon ground allspice
- 1   teaspoon *each* ground cumin and ground coriander
- 2   teaspoons dry oregano leaves
- 1   large can (about 28 oz.) kidney beans, drained
     Plain yogurt
     Fresh cilantro (coriander) leaves

Pour oil into a 3-quart microwave-safe casserole; tip casserole to coat bottom evenly with oil. Crumble turkey into casserole; microwave, uncovered, on **HIGH (100%)** for 6 minutes, stirring after 3 minutes. Stir in onion and microwave, uncovered, on **HIGH (100%)** for 3 minutes; then add chiles, broth, tomatoes (break up with a spoon) and their liquid, allspice, cumin, ground coriander, and oregano.

Cover and microwave on **HIGH (100%)** for 10 minutes, stirring after 5 minutes. Stir in beans. Microwave, uncovered, on **HIGH (100%)** for 15 to 20 minutes or until chili is bubbly all over, stirring after 7 to 8 minutes. Let stand, covered, for 5 minutes.

To serve, ladle chili into bowls. Offer yogurt and cilantro to add to individual servings. Makes 4 servings.

Per serving: 408 calories, 28 g protein, 38 g carbohydrates, 17 g total fat, 76 mg cholesterol, 1,622 mg sodium

Pictured on page 10

CHUNKY CONDIMENT CHILI

✳   ✳   ✳   ✳   ✳   ✳   ✳   ✳

Preparation time: 15 to 20 minutes
Microwaving time: 20 to 25 minutes
Standing time: 5 minutes

Start with a basic no-bean chili, then add your choice of flavorful toppings to create the dish that's just right for you.

- 1 pound lean ground beef
- 1 medium-size onion, chopped
- 1 clove garlic, minced or pressed
- ½ medium-size red bell pepper, seeded and diced
- 1 large can (28 oz.) tomatoes
- 2 tablespoons chili powder
- 3 whole cloves
- 1 teaspoon ground cumin
- 1 small can (about 8 oz.) whole-kernel corn, drained
  Fresh cilantro (coriander) sprigs (optional)
  Condiments (suggestions follow)

Crumble beef into a 3- to 4-quart microwave-safe casserole. Microwave, uncovered, on **HIGH (100%)** for 5 minutes, stirring after 2½ minutes. Add onion and garlic; microwave, uncovered, on **HIGH (100%)** for 5 minutes, stirring after 2½ minutes. Stir in bell pepper, tomatoes (break up with a spoon) and their liquid, chili powder, cloves, cumin, and corn. Cover and microwave on **HIGH (100%)** for 10 to 15 minutes or until chili is bubbly all over, stirring every 4 to 5 minutes. Let stand, covered, for 5 minutes.

Ladle chili into bowls; garnish with cilantro, if desired. Offer condiments to top individual servings. Makes 4 servings.

Condiments. Present 3 or 4 of the following in individual bowls: shredded **Cheddar cheese, plain yogurt** or sour cream, sliced **green onions** (including tops), **fresh cilantro (coriander) leaves, tortilla chips** or corn chips, and **avocado** cubes.

Per serving (without condiments): 408 calories, 24 g protein, 24 g carbohydrates, 25 g total fat, 85 mg cholesterol, 596 mg sodium

CHINESE CHICKEN & SHRIMP SOUP

✳   ✳   ✳   ✳   ✳   ✳   ✳   ✳

Preparation time: About 25 minutes
Microwaving time: 15 to 20 minutes
Standing time: 2 minutes

Delicate but nourishing, this soup makes a satisfying light supper. For a heartier dish, stir hot cooked rice into the soup just before serving.

- 6 cups regular-strength chicken broth
- 2 tablespoons finely chopped fresh ginger
- 2 to 3 teaspoons soy sauce
- ½ pound mushrooms, sliced
- 1 cup diced firm tofu (bean curd)
- ½ cup sliced green onions (including tops)
- 1 whole chicken breast (about 1 lb.), skinned, boned, and cut into ½-inch cubes
- 3 cups thinly sliced bok choy
- ½ pound tiny cooked and shelled shrimp
- ¼ cup chopped fresh cilantro (coriander)
  Ground red pepper (cayenne) or chili oil (optional)

Combine broth, ginger, soy, mushrooms, tofu, and onions in a 3½- to 4-quart microwave-safe casserole. Cover and microwave on **HIGH (100%)** for 10 to 12 minutes or until broth is steaming, stirring after 5 minutes. Stir in chicken and bok choy, cover, and microwave on **HIGH (100%)** for 5 to 8 minutes or until chicken is no longer pink in center (cut to test) and broth begins to boil; stir after 4 minutes. Add shrimp and cilantro, then cover and let stand for 2 minutes. Season to taste with red pepper, if desired. Makes 4 servings.

Per serving: 307 calories, 45 g protein, 11 g carbohydrates, 11 g total fat, 153 mg cholesterol, 1,942 mg sodium

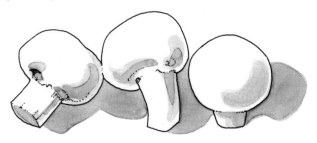

CURRIED CHICKEN SOUP

Preparation time: About 20 minutes
Microwaving time: 21 to 23 minutes
Standing time: 3 minutes

If you cook this soup in a tureen or decorative casserole, it's ready to go to the table the instant you take it from the microwave. To dress up individual portions, offer condiments at the table.

1 tablespoon butter or margarine
1 small onion, chopped
2 teaspoons curry powder
½ teaspoon ground ginger
1 whole chicken breast (about 1 lb.), skinned, boned, and cut into ½-inch cubes
2 cans (14½ oz. *each*) regular-strength chicken broth
2 cups frozen peas, thawed
1 medium-size Red Delicious apple, cored and diced
1 teaspoon sugar
2 tablespoons chopped fresh cilantro (coriander)
    Condiments (suggestions follow)

Place butter in a 3½- to 4-quart microwave-safe casserole or soup tureen. Microwave, uncovered, on **HIGH (100%)** for about 30 seconds or until melted. Stir in onion, curry powder, and ginger. Cover and microwave on **HIGH (100%)** for 4 minutes. Stir in chicken, cover, and microwave on **HIGH (100%)** for 6 minutes. Stir in broth, peas, apple, and sugar. Cover and microwave on **HIGH (100%)** for 10 to 12 minutes or until bubbly, stirring every 4 minutes. Let stand, covered, for 3 minutes; then garnish with cilantro. Offer condiments to add to individual servings. Makes about 4 servings.

Condiments. Offer individual bowls of hot **cooked rice, salted roasted almonds, raisins,** and **sweetened or unsweetened shredded coconut.**

Per serving (without condiments): 229 calories, 23 g protein, 21 g carbohydrates, 6 g total fat, 51 mg cholesterol, 1,069 mg sodium

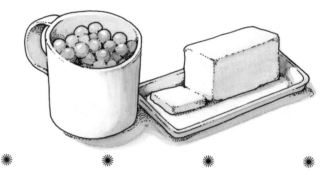

SAUSAGE SOUP OLÉ

Preparation time: About 15 minutes
Microwaving time: 22 to 24 minutes
Standing time: 3 minutes

Laden with vegetables and chunks of sausage, this tantalizing soup tastes like it's been simmering all day—but the microwave lets you cook it in well under an hour.

1 pound bulk pork sausage
1½ cups thinly sliced carrots
1 envelope dry onion soup mix (enough for 4 cups soup)
5 cups hot water
1 can (1 lb.) small whole onions, drained
1 can (about 1 lb.) kidney beans, drained
1 can (about 1 lb.) stewed tomatoes
1 can (about 1 lb.) baby corn on the cob, drained
1 teaspoon dry oregano leaves
½ teaspoon ground cumin
    Condiments (suggestions follow)

Crumble sausage into a 4- to 5-quart microwave-safe casserole or soup tureen. Cover and microwave on **HIGH (100%)** for 6 minutes, stirring every 2 minutes. Drain off and discard all fat. Stir in carrots, soup mix, and 1 cup of the hot water. Cover and microwave on **HIGH (100%)** for 8 to 10 minutes or until carrots are tender when pierced, stirring after 4 minutes. Add onions, beans, tomatoes, corn, oregano, cumin, and remaining 4 cups hot water. Cover and microwave on **HIGH (100%)** for 8 minutes or until steaming, stirring every 3 minutes. Let stand, covered, for 3 minutes.

Ladle soup into individual bowls; offer condiments to add to taste. Makes 8 servings.

Condiments. Offer individual bowls of thinly sliced **green onions** (including tops), **sour cream, avocado** cubes or slices, **green chile salsa** or taco sauce, and **lime** wedges.

Per serving (without condiments): 200 calories, 9 g protein, 21 g carbohydrates, 9 g total fat, 23 mg cholesterol, 1,267 mg sodium

Here's one hearty company meal you can't improve on—red wine, crusty French bread, and big bowls of steaming San Francisco-style Cioppino (recipe on page 17). Clams, shrimp, and cracked crab in a savory tomato broth make a stew that's as satisfying as it is quick to cook.

CALIFORNIA CORN CHOWDER

Preparation time: 10 to 15 minutes
Microwaving time: 30 to 33 minutes
Standing time: 3 minutes

Sparked with diced green chiles, this creamy soup is ready to enjoy in about 45 minutes. While it cooks, toss a green salad; then bring out a basket of bread sticks, and dinner is served!

　　2　slices bacon, diced
　　2　mild Italian sausages (about 7 oz. *total*), cut into thin slices
　　1　medium-size onion, chopped
　　1　medium-size red thin-skinned potato, diced
　⅓　cup water
　　1　can (about 1 lb.) cream-style corn
　　2　to 3 tablespoons canned diced green chiles
　　1　jar (2 oz.) sliced pimentos, drained
　　2　cups milk
　　　Garlic salt and pepper

Distribute bacon pieces over bottom of a 3-quart microwave-safe casserole. Cover and microwave on **HIGH (100%)** for 3 minutes or until bacon is crisp; lift bacon from casserole with a slotted spoon and set aside. Pour off and discard drippings.

Add sausages and onion to casserole; cover and microwave on **HIGH (100%)** for 6 minutes, stirring after 3 minutes. Stir in potato and water; cover and microwave on **HIGH (100%)** for 9 minutes or until potato is tender when pierced, stirring every 3 minutes. Stir in corn, chiles, pimentos, and milk.

Cover and microwave on **HIGH (100%)** for 12 to 15 minutes or until steaming, stirring every 4 minutes. Season to taste with garlic salt and pepper. Cover and let stand for 3 minutes.

To serve, ladle soup into individual bowls. Top each serving with bacon. Makes 3 servings.

Per serving: 552 calories, 22 g protein, 48 g carbohydrates, 32 g total fat, 84 mg cholesterol, 1,184 mg sodium

LAMB COUSCOUS

Preparation time: About 20 minutes
Microwaving time: 46 minutes
Standing time: 5 minutes

Our microwave version of the famous one-dish Moroccan meal features tender lamb and vegetables spiced up with a zesty seasoning sauce.

　1½　pounds lean boneless lamb shoulder
　　1　medium-size onion, chopped
　　2　large carrots, cut into 1-inch-thick slices
　¼　teaspoon black pepper
　　1　can (14½ oz.) regular-strength chicken broth
　　　Steamed Couscous (recipe follows)
　　1　small red bell pepper, seeded and diced
　　1　small can (about 8 oz.) garbanzo beans, drained
　　1　can (about 14 oz.) artichoke hearts in water, drained
　　　Seasoning Sauce (recipe follows)

Trim and discard excess fat from lamb, then cut lamb into 1-inch cubes. Place in a 4-quart microwave-safe casserole. Microwave, uncovered, on **HIGH (100%)** for 7 minutes, stirring after 3 minutes. Stir in onion, carrots, black pepper, and 1 cup of the broth (reserve remainder for Steamed Cous-

cous). Cover and microwave on **HIGH (100%)** for 5 minutes. Stir; cover and microwave on **MEDIUM (50%)** for 25 minutes or until meat is tender when pierced, stirring every 10 minutes. Cover; set aside.

Prepare Steamed Couscous; set aside. Stir bell pepper, garbanzos, and artichokes into lamb mixture; cover and microwave on **HIGH (100%)** for 5 minutes. Prepare Seasoning Sauce, stir into lamb mixture, cover, and let stand for 5 minutes.

Fluff couscous with a fork. Mound on a platter; top with lamb mixture. Makes 4 servings.

Steamed Couscous. Add enough **water** to **remaining chicken broth** to make 1½ cups liquid. Pour into a 2½- to 3-quart microwave-safe casserole. Add 1 tablespoon **butter** or margarine, ¼ cup **raisins,** and a dash of **ground cinnamon.** Cover; microwave on **HIGH (100%)** for 4 minutes or until boiling. Stir in 1½ cups **couscous;** cover.

Seasoning Sauce. In a small bowl, stir together 2 tablespoons **catsup,** ¼ teaspoon **liquid hot pepper seasoning,** ½ teaspoon **ground cumin,** ¼ teaspoon **ground nutmeg**, and ⅛ teaspoon **ground cloves.**

Per serving: 628 calories, 46 g protein, 75 g carbohydrates, 17 g total fat, 120 mg cholesterol, 929 mg sodium

PRUNE-GLAZED PORK STEW

Preparation time: 15 to 20 minutes
Microwaving time: 18 to 20 minutes
Standing time: 3 to 5 minutes

Pork butt is usually a good buy at the market, and it cooks quickly to juicy tenderness in the microwave. Team it with peas and prunes in a spicy, speedy stew to serve over rice.

1¼	to 1½ pounds lean boneless pork butt
1	medium-size onion, chopped
1	clove garlic, minced or pressed
½	cup prune juice
1½	teaspoons lemon juice
½	teaspoon dry rosemary
¼	teaspoon *each* ground cinnamon, ground ginger, and pepper
2	teaspoons cornstarch mixed with 1 tablespoon water
1¼	cups frozen peas, thawed
12	to 16 pitted prunes
	Salt
	Hot cooked rice

Trim and discard excess fat from pork; then cut pork into 1-inch cubes and place in a 10-inch square or 8- by 12-inch microwave-safe baking dish. Cover and microwave on **HIGH (100%)** for 5 minutes, stirring after 3 minutes. Add onion and garlic. Cover and microwave on **HIGH (100%)** for 7 minutes or until meat is tender when pierced, stirring every 2 to 3 minutes. Drain off cooking liquid into a 4-cup glass measure; cover meat mixture and set aside.

Skim and discard fat from cooking liquid; then stir in prune juice, lemon juice, rosemary, cinnamon, ginger, pepper, and cornstarch mixture. Microwave, uncovered, on **HIGH (100%)** for 4 minutes or until sauce is thickened and clear, stirring after 2 minutes.

Pour sauce over meat mixture and stir in peas and prunes; then cover and microwave on **HIGH (100%)** for 2 to 4 minutes or until bubbly, stirring after 2 minutes. Season to taste with salt; cover and let stand for 3 to 5 minutes. Serve over rice. Makes 4 servings.

Per serving: 401 calories, 33 g protein, 34 g carbohydrates, 15 g total fat, 106 mg cholesterol, 164 mg sodium

Pictured on page 15

SAN FRANCISCO–STYLE CIOPPINO

Preparation time: About 20 minutes
Microwaving time: 20 to 21 minutes
Standing time: 5 minutes

Legend has it that this robust shellfish stew was invented by an Italian fisherman in San Francisco. Though a bit messy to eat, it's definitely company fare—just be sure to have plenty of napkins handy.

1	tablespoon olive oil or salad oil
1	medium-size onion, chopped
1	large clove garlic, minced or pressed
½	large green bell pepper, seeded and diced
1	can (8 oz.) tomato sauce
1	can (about 1 lb.) stewed tomatoes
½	cup dry white wine
1	dry bay leaf
1	teaspoon dry basil
½	teaspoon dry oregano leaves
¼	cup chopped parsley

⅓	pound medium-large raw shrimp (31 to 35 per lb.), shelled and deveined
1	cooked Dungeness or other hard-shell crab (about 1½ lbs.), cleaned and cracked
8	small hard-shell clams in shell, suitable for steaming, scrubbed

Pour oil into a 3-quart microwave-safe casserole; tip casserole to coat bottom evenly with oil. Add onion, garlic, and bell pepper; cover and microwave on **HIGH (100%)** for 5 minutes, stirring after 2½ minutes. Stir in tomato sauce, tomatoes, wine, bay leaf, basil, oregano, and parsley. Cover and microwave on **HIGH (100%)** for 10 minutes, stirring every 3 minutes. Add shrimp, crab, and clams. Cover and microwave on **HIGH (100%)** for 5 to 6 minutes or until clams have opened. Let stand, covered, for 5 minutes. Makes about 4 servings.

Per serving: 186 calories, 20 g protein, 16 g carbohydrates, 5 g total fat, 96 mg cholesterol, 809 mg sodium

*Recipe for the perfect weekend brunch: sunny weather, fresh flowers
on the table, and Cream Cheese Eggs with Smoked Salmon (recipe on page 20)
on the menu. Complement the rich, fluffy eggs with toasted bagels
and your choice of fruit.*

Eggs, Cheese & Pasta

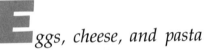**E**ggs, cheese, and pasta are great for quick and easy dinners even when traditional cooking methods are used. But when you make these entrées in the microwave, you not only save time, you spare yourself a lot of dishwashing. In fact, almost all our recipes—from scrambled eggs to creamy fondue to an old-fashioned chicken-noodle casserole—are cooked and served in one dish. We begin with some egg-based favorites, then go on to tempting cheese dishes. At the end of the chapter, you'll find a selection of pasta specialties.

Pictured on page 18

CREAM CHEESE EGGS WITH SMOKED SALMON

✳   ✳   ✳   ✳   ✳   ✳   ✳

Preparation time: 5 to 10 minutes
Microwaving time: About 5 minutes
Standing time: 1 minute

Strips of green onion and bright pink smoked salmon add color and flavor to this elegant egg dish; chunks of cream cheese give it a moist, fluffy texture.

2 tablespoons butter or margarine
8 large eggs
¼ pound thinly sliced smoked salmon or lox, cut into 1-inch-long pieces
2 green onions (including tops), thinly sliced
1 small package (3 oz.) cream cheese, cut into ½-inch cubes

Place butter in a 1½-quart microwave-safe casserole. Microwave, uncovered, on **HIGH (100%)** for about 35 seconds. Break eggs into dish and beat with a wire whisk until blended. Microwave, uncovered, on **HIGH (100%)** for 2½ minutes; stir every minute to bring cooked eggs to inside of dish and allow uncooked portion to flow to edges. Reserve a few salmon strips and some of the onions for garnish; add remaining salmon and onions and all the cream cheese cubes to eggs. Stir to blend.

Microwave, uncovered, on **HIGH (100%)** for 1½ minutes, stirring after 45 seconds. Let stand, uncovered, for 1 minute. Garnish with reserved salmon and onions. Makes about 4 servings.

Per serving: 309 calories, 19 g protein, 2 g carbohydrates, 24 g total fat, 470 mg cholesterol, 470 mg sodium

JOE'S EGGS

✳   ✳   ✳   ✳   ✳   ✳   ✳

Preparation time: 15 to 20 minutes
Microwaving time: 20 minutes
Standing time: 1 minute

Here's a microwave take-off on "Joe's Special," an old San Francisco favorite that combines eggs, ground beef, and fresh spinach. To complete the meal, just add sourdough bread and a mixed green salad with Caesar-style dressing.

1 pound lean ground beef
1 large onion, finely chopped
1 clove garlic, minced or pressed
¼ pound mushrooms, thinly sliced
¼ teaspoon *each* ground nutmeg, pepper, and dry oregano leaves
6 cups lightly packed torn spinach leaves
8 large eggs
  Salt
1 cup (4 oz.) shredded jack cheese

Crumble beef into a shallow 3-quart microwave-safe baking dish. Add onion, garlic, mushrooms, nutmeg, pepper, and oregano. Microwave, uncovered, on **HIGH (100%)** for 9 minutes or until beef is no longer pink and onion is soft; stir every 3 minutes during cooking. Spoon off and discard all liquid.

Set spinach on top of beef mixture; cover and microwave on **HIGH (100%)** for 3 minutes. In a bowl, beat eggs until blended; add to mixture in baking dish. Microwave, uncovered, on **HIGH (100%)** for 8 minutes, stirring every 2 minutes to bring cooked eggs to inside of dish and allow uncooked portion to flow to edges. Season to taste with salt. Sprinkle with cheese. Let stand, uncovered, for 1 minute; eggs should be softly set. Makes 6 servings.

Per serving: 347 calories, 29 g protein, 6 g carbohydrates, 23 g total fat, 343 mg cholesterol, 262 mg sodium

MICROWAVE

BASICS

FOR EGGS

For successfully cooked eggs, keep two important precautions in mind. First, pay close attention to timing—mere seconds can make all the difference. Second, NEVER microwave an egg in its shell.

Because egg yolks have a higher fat content than egg whites, they absorb more microwave energy and cook more quickly than whites do. For this reason, it's important to stir scrambled eggs for even cooking and to puncture the fine membrane over the yolk of an egg to be poached or fried (to prevent explosion).

On this page, we present basic methods for poaching, frying, and scrambling eggs in a microwave oven. *We did our testing with large eggs.*

POACHED EGGS

Success with microwave-poached eggs depends on attention to two rules. To start with, make sure the water has reached a *full* boil, with bubbles breaking the surface, before you add the eggs. And never forget to prick the membrane over each yolk.

For 1 egg, pour ¼ cup hot water and ¼ teaspoon white vinegar into a 10-ounce microwave-safe custard cup. Microwave, uncovered, on **HIGH (100%)** for 1½ minutes or until water reaches a full boil. Carefully break 1 egg into boiling water. With a fork, prick egg yolk straight down through membrane; cover cup and microwave on **HIGH (100%)** for 40 seconds. Remove from oven and let stand, covered, for 2 minutes. For a firmer egg, let stand for 3 to 4 more minutes. To serve, lift egg from water with a slotted spoon.

For 2 eggs, proceed as above, cooking each egg in its own custard cup; cooking time is the same.

For 3 or 4 eggs, measure water and vinegar into custard cups and arrange in a circle on a flat 12-inch microwave-safe plate (this makes it easy to remove the eggs from the oven quickly). Proceed as above, allowing 3½ to 4 minutes for the water in the cups to reach a full boil. For 3 eggs, allow 1½ to 2 minutes of cooking time; for 4 eggs, allow 2 to 2½ minutes.

FRIED EGGS

To fry eggs in the microwave, you'll need a browning dish. It's also best to fry no more than 2 eggs at a time.

Preheat a 2- to 2½-quart or 10-inch square microwave browning dish on **HIGH (100%)** for 2 minutes. Using oven mitts, carefully remove dish to a heatproof surface. Add 1 teaspoon butter or margarine per egg to hot dish; tilt dish to coat bottom with butter. Carefully break 1 or 2 eggs into dish. With a fork, prick egg yolks straight down through membrane. Cover with a glass lid. Microwave on **HIGH (100%)** for 35 to 45 seconds per egg (if cooking 2 eggs, give dish a quarter-turn after 30 seconds). Remove from oven; let stand, covered, for 2 to 3 minutes before serving.

FLUFFY SCRAMBLED EGGS

Scrambled eggs should still be moist when you remove them from the oven—they'll continue to cook briefly as they stand. If, after standing, they are moister than you like, microwave them for 15 to 30 more seconds. We recommend scrambling no more than 8 eggs at a time in the microwave.

Our recipe uses butter for flavor only. If you prefer to omit butter, do so—the eggs will cook quite successfully without it.

For each egg, place butter or margarine in a dish of the correct size as directed below; you might use microwave-safe custard cups or small casseroles. Microwave, uncovered, on **HIGH (100%)** for 30 to 35 seconds or until butter is melted. Break eggs into dish. Add milk and beat with a wire whisk until well blended. Microwave, uncovered, on **HIGH (100%)** for time given in chart below, stirring every minute to bring cooked portion to center of dish. Let eggs stand for 1 to 2 minutes before serving.

Container	Butter or Margarine	Eggs	Milk or Water	Cooking Time
10 oz.	2 tsp.	2	2 Tbsp.	1¼–1½ min.
1 qt.	1 Tbsp.	4	3 Tbsp.	2½–3¼ min.
1 qt.	1½ Tbsp.	6	¼ cup	3½–4¼ min.
1½ qt.	2 Tbsp.	8	⅓ cup	4½–5¼ min.

ROLLED CORN FRITTATA

❋ ❋ ❋ ❋ ❋ ❋ ❋

Preparation time: 5 to 10 minutes
Microwaving time: About 7 minutes
Standing time: 1 minute

To make this Italian-style omelet, you briefly microwave fresh corn kernels, diced red pepper, and green onion in a pie plate, then pour in beaten eggs and cook just until the eggs are softly set.

2 tablespoons butter or margarine
¾ cup fresh corn kernels (about 1 medium-size ear); or ¾ cup frozen corn kernels, thawed
½ cup diced red or green bell pepper
⅓ cup chopped green onions (including tops)
4 large eggs
2 tablespoons whipping cream or milk
⅛ teaspoon liquid hot pepper seasoning
Salt

Place butter in a 9-inch microwave-safe pie plate. Microwave, uncovered, on **HIGH (100%)** for about 35 seconds. Stir in corn, bell pepper, and onions. Microwave, uncovered, on **HIGH (100%)** for 3 minutes, stirring after 1½ minutes.

Break eggs into pie plate; add cream and hot pepper seasoning. Beat with a wire whisk until blended. Microwave, uncovered, on **HIGH (100%)** for 1½ minutes. Remove plate from microwave; gently lift cooked eggs, tipping plate to let uncooked portion flow to edges. Then microwave, uncovered, on **HIGH (100%)** for 1½ minutes or until eggs are softly set but still moist. Let stand, uncovered, for 1 minute. Then tilt plate and roll or fold frittata out onto a serving plate. Season to taste with salt. Makes 2 servings.

Per serving: 354 calories, 15 g protein, 15 g carbohydrates, 27 g total fat, 473 mg cholesterol, 267 mg sodium

Pictured on facing page

ASPARAGUS & HAM STRATA

❋ ❋ ❋ ❋ ❋ ❋ ❋

Preparation time: 15 to 20 minutes
Chilling time: At least 8 hours
Microwaving time: 21 minutes
Standing time: 10 minutes

Puffy and soufflélike, this casserole goes together a day ahead, then waits overnight in the refrigerator until you're ready to cook and serve it.

¾ pound asparagus
2 tablespoons water
2 tablespoons butter or margarine, at room temperature
4 slices firm-textured white bread
1¾ cups (7 oz.) shredded Cheddar cheese
1 cup diced cooked ham
4 large eggs
1½ tablespoons instant minced onion
½ teaspoon *each* dry mustard and Worcestershire
¼ teaspoon *each* garlic powder and ground red pepper (cayenne)
1⅓ cups half-and-half

Snap off and discard tough ends of asparagus, then cut stalks into 1-inch pieces and place in a 9-inch square microwave-safe baking dish. Add water;

cover and microwave on **HIGH (100%)** for 5 minutes, stirring after 2 minutes to bring outside pieces to center. Drain asparagus and set aside.

Wipe baking dish dry, then evenly coat bottom and sides with 1½ teaspoons of the butter. Spread remaining 1½ tablespoons butter over both sides of bread slices. Arrange bread in an even layer in baking dish; top evenly with 1¼ cups of the cheese, then with ham and asparagus.

In a small bowl, beat eggs until blended. Mix in onion, mustard, Worcestershire, garlic powder, red pepper, and half-and-half. Pour egg mixture evenly over layered ingredients in baking dish. Cover and refrigerate for at least 8 hours or until next day.

To cook, microwave, uncovered, on **MEDIUM-HIGH (70–80%)** for 10 minutes, giving dish a half-turn after 5 minutes. Then microwave on **HIGH (100%)** for 3 minutes; give dish a half-turn and evenly sprinkle strata with remaining ½ cup cheese. Microwave, uncovered, on **HIGH (100%)** for 3 more minutes. Let stand, uncovered, for 10 minutes; strata should feel firm in center when lightly touched. To serve, cut into squares. Makes about 6 servings.

Per serving: 383 calories, 22 g protein, 13 g carbohydrates, 27 g total fat, 221 mg cholesterol, 754 mg sodium

Toast the springtime with sparkling champagne and colorful
Asparagus & Ham Strata (recipe on facing page). You assemble the casserole
a day ahead; to serve, just microwave for about 15 minutes—and a
full-flavored lunch, brunch, or supper is on the table!

FRESH PASTA
IN THE
MICROWAVE

Hot pasta plus a simple sauce is a long-time favorite for dinner in a hurry. And with the help of your microwave, such spur-of-the-moment suppers become faster and easier still. Fresh pasta from your supermarket's delicatessen or refrigerator case can be cooked in a few inches of water—there's no need to boil up a big pot full. Homemade sauces, too, can be prepared in a jiffy.

Here, we give directions for microwaving all types of fresh pasta, from thin angel hair to more robust tortellini and ravioli. To top the pasta, take your choice of three sauces: meaty Neapolitan Tomato Sauce, creamy Four-cheese Sauce, and fresh-tasting Basil-Parmesan Sauce.

ZAPPED PASTA & SAUCES

Preparation time: About 15 minutes
Microwaving time: 20 to 27 minutes

Mix and match pasta and sauces to suit your taste.

- **2 packages (9 oz. *each*) fresh pasta, such as angel hair pasta, linguine, fettuccine, tortellini, or ravioli**
- **2½ cups very hot water**
  Neapolitan Tomato Sauce, Four-cheese Sauce, or Basil-Parmesan Sauce (recipes follow)
  Freshly grated Parmesan cheese

Arrange pasta of your choice evenly in a 2½- to 3-quart microwave-safe casserole or baking dish. Pour hot water over pasta; push pasta down into water. Cover and microwave on **HIGH (100%)** for 8 to 10 minutes or just until tender to bite, stirring after 5 minutes. Drain off water.

Prepare sauce of your choice; pour hot sauce evenly over pasta in casserole. Cover and microwave on **HIGH (100%)** for 2 to 4 minutes or until pasta is heated through. Pass cheese to sprinkle over individual servings. Makes 4 to 6 servings.

Neapolitan Tomato Sauce. Crumble 1 pound **Italian sausages** (casings removed) or 1 pound lean ground beef into a shallow 2- to 2½-quart microwave-safe baking dish. Cover and microwave on **HIGH (100%)** for 3 minutes, stirring after 1½ minutes. Drain off fat. To sausage, add ¼ pound **mushrooms,** sliced, and 1 clove **garlic,** minced or pressed. Cover and microwave on **HIGH (100%)** for 3 to 5 minutes or until mushrooms are soft, stirring after 2 minutes. Blend in 3 cups **prepared spaghetti sauce** and ⅓ cup **dry red wine.** Cover and microwave on **HIGH (100%)** for about 5 minutes or until sauce is very hot and bubbly, stirring every 2 to 3 minutes. Makes about 4 cups.

Four-cheese Sauce. Place ¼ cup **butter** or margarine in a 1- to 1½-quart microwave-safe casserole or bowl. Microwave, uncovered, on **HIGH (100%)** for about 45 seconds or until butter is melted. Stir in 1½ tablespoons **all-purpose flour,** ⅛ to ¼ teaspoon **ground nutmeg,** and a dash of **ground white pepper.** Gradually stir in 1 cup **half-and-half** and ½ cup **regular-strength chicken broth** to make a smooth mixture. Microwave, uncovered, on **HIGH (100%)** for 5 minutes, stirring after 3 minutes. Stir sauce well; then microwave, uncovered, on **HIGH (100%)** for 3 minutes or until sauce boils and thickens, stirring every minute.

Mix in ⅓ cup shredded **Swiss or fontina cheese** and ⅓ cup shredded **Havarti, Bel Paese, or Münster cheese;** microwave, uncovered, on **HIGH (100%)** for 1 minute or until cheese is melted. Stir in ⅓ cup crumbled **blue-veined cheese** and ½ cup freshly grated **Parmesan cheese.** Makes about 3½ cups.

Basil-Parmesan Sauce. In a food processor, combine ¾ cup lightly packed **fresh basil leaves** (rinsed and patted dry) and ½ cup freshly grated **Parmesan cheese.** Whirl, using on-and-off bursts, until mixture looks like green sawdust. Set aside.

Place 3 tablespoons **butter** or margarine in a 1- to 1½-quart microwave-safe casserole or bowl. Microwave, uncovered, on **HIGH (100%)** for about 40 seconds or until butter is melted. Stir in 1½ tablespoons **all-purpose flour;** gradually stir in 1 cup **half-and-half** and ½ cup **regular-strength chicken broth** to make a smooth mixture. Microwave, uncovered, on **HIGH (100%)** for 5 minutes, stirring after 3 minutes. Stir sauce well; then microwave, uncovered, on **HIGH (100%)** for 3 minutes or until sauce boils and thickens, stirring every minute.

Stir in basil-Parmesan mixture until well blended. Season to taste with **salt.** Makes about 3½ cups.

Per serving with angel hair pasta and Neapolitan Tomato Sauce: 681 calories, 29 g protein, 82 g carbohydrates, 27 g total fat, 172 mg cholesterol, 1,383 mg sodium

Per serving with angel hair pasta and Four-cheese Sauce: 581 calories, 25 g protein, 61 g carbohydrates, 27 g total fat, 192 mg cholesterol, 622 mg sodium

Per serving with angel hair pasta and Basil-Parmesan Sauce: 484 calories, 19 g protein, 62 g carbohydrates, 18 g total fat, 164 mg cholesterol, 400 mg sodium

CRUSTLESS SEAFOOD QUICHE

Preparation time: 5 to 10 minutes
Microwaving time: 10 to 11 minutes
Standing time: 10 minutes

Once you eliminate the crust, a quiche is a natural candidate for microwave cooking. This version can be prepared with crab or tuna.

1	tablespoon butter or margarine, at room temperature
½	pound cooked crabmeat or 1 can (9¼ oz.) tuna packed in water, drained
1	cup (4 oz.) shredded Swiss cheese
¼	cup *each* grated Parmesan cheese and sliced green onions (including tops)
1	jar (2 oz.) diced pimentos, drained
3	large eggs
1	cup half-and-half
¼	teaspoon *each* salt and ground nutmeg
⅛	teaspoon ground red pepper (cayenne)

Evenly spread butter over bottom and sides of a 9-inch microwave-safe pie plate or 10-inch quiche dish. Distribute crab evenly over bottom of plate. Then sprinkle crab evenly with Swiss cheese, Parmesan cheese, onions, and pimentos. Set aside.

In a 4-cup glass measure, beat eggs until blended. Mix in half-and-half, salt, nutmeg, and red pepper. Cover egg mixture and microwave on **HIGH (100%)** for 3 minutes, stirring after 1½ minutes. Beat egg mixture to blend, then pour evenly over layered ingredients in pie plate. Shake plate to distribute egg mixture evenly.

Microwave, uncovered, on **HIGH (100%)** for 7 to 8 minutes, giving dish a quarter-turn every 2 minutes. Let stand, uncovered, for 10 minutes; quiche should feel firm in center when gently touched. To serve, cut into wedges. Makes about 6 servings.

Per serving: 235 calories, 19 g protein, 4 g carbohydrates, 16 g total fat, 184 mg cholesterol, 377 mg sodium

CHILE EGG PUFF

Preparation time: 5 minutes
Microwaving time: About 13 minutes
Standing time: 10 minutes

Sturdier than a soufflé but lighter than scrambled eggs, this casserole of eggs, chiles, and two cheeses is sure to become a family favorite. If you like, offer picante sauce to spoon over individual portions.

¼	cup butter or margarine
6	large eggs
¼	cup all-purpose flour
½	teaspoon baking powder
¼	teaspoon salt
1	cup small-curd cottage cheese
2	cups (8 oz.) shredded jack cheese
1	can (4 oz.) diced green chiles
	About 1 cup homemade or purchased picante sauce (optional)

Place butter in a shallow 2-quart microwave-safe baking dish. Microwave on **HIGH (100%)** for about 45 seconds or until butter is melted. Break eggs into dish and beat with a wire whisk until blended. Then mix in flour, baking powder, salt, cottage cheese, 1½ cups of the jack cheese, and chiles until blended. Smooth to make an even layer.

Microwave, uncovered, on **MEDIUM-HIGH (70–80%)** for 5 minutes. Remove dish from oven and stir, bringing cooked edges of mixture toward center of dish and allowing uncooked portion to flow to edges. Then microwave, uncovered, on **MEDIUM-HIGH (70–80%)** for 5 more minutes, giving dish a half-turn after 2½ minutes. Sprinkle egg puff with remaining ½ cup jack cheese. Microwave, uncovered, on **HIGH (100%)** for 2 minutes or until cheese is melted and puff appears barely set in center. Let stand, uncovered, for 10 minutes; puff should feel firm in center when lightly touched. Offer picante sauce to spoon over individual portions, if desired. Makes about 6 servings.

Per serving: 346 calories, 21 g protein, 7 g carbohydrates, 26 g total fat, 272 mg cholesterol, 738 mg sodium

*Simply irresistible! When you bring out Mexican Baked Cheese with
Shrimp (recipe on facing page), everyone will want to dig right in. Let diners
use warm corn tortillas to enclose the bubbly melted cheese and its
toppings of tiny shrimp and chile-tomato salsa.*

EGG & CHEESE TORTILLA ROLL-UPS

Preparation time: About 10 minutes
Microwaving time: 14 to 18 minutes

To make these quick "sandwiches," break an egg onto a hot tortilla, embellish with cheese and bits of crisp chorizo, and microwave briefly. Then simply roll up and eat out of hand.

½ pound chorizo sausage, casings removed
8 flour tortillas (*each* about 8 inches in diameter)
8 large eggs
2 cups (8 oz.) shredded Cheddar cheese
8 green onions, roots and tops trimmed (*each* trimmed onion should be 8 inches long)
2 medium-size ripe tomatoes, thinly sliced
1 can (4 oz.) whole green chiles, seeded and cut into ½-inch-wide strips

Crumble chorizo into an 8- or 9-inch microwave-safe pie plate; cover with a paper towel. Microwave on **HIGH (100%)** for 4 minutes, stirring after 2 minutes. With a slotted spoon, lift chorizo from pie plate and set aside. Wipe plate clean.

To make each roll-up, place a tortilla in pie plate. Microwave, uncovered, on **HIGH (100%)** for 15 seconds. Break an egg onto tortilla; prick egg yolk with a fork, then gently stir to distribute egg evenly. Sprinkle with ¼ cup of the cheese and an eighth of the chorizo. Cover loosely, then microwave on **HIGH (100%)** for 1 to 1½ minutes or until egg is barely set. Slide onto a plate; quickly add 1 onion, a few tomato slices, and a few chile strips. Roll up tortilla.

Repeat with remaining tortillas, eggs, and toppings. Makes 4 servings (2 tortillas *each*).

Per serving: 749 calories, 42 g protein, 58 g carbohydrates, 38 g total fat, 516 mg cholesterol, 1,248 mg sodium

---

Pictured on facing page

MEXICAN BAKED CHEESE WITH SHRIMP

Preparation time: About 10 minutes
Microwaving time: About 22 minutes

Topped with a cinnamon- and chile-sparked salsa, thick slices of cheese turn soft and creamy in the microwave. Scoop the hot mixture onto warm corn tortillas to serve.

1½ tablespoons olive oil or salad oil
1 medium-size onion, finely chopped
2 medium-size tomatoes, seeded and coarsely chopped
¼ teaspoon ground cinnamon
4 to 8 small fresh or canned jalapeño chiles, seeded and minced
Salt
1½ pounds mild cheese, such as Münster, jack, teleme, fontina, Edam, or Gouda
½ pound tiny cooked and shelled shrimp
12 corn or flour tortillas (*each* 6 to 8 inches in diameter), heated

Place oil in a 2-quart microwave-safe baking dish. Microwave, uncovered, on **HIGH (100%)** for 1½ minutes. Add onion; microwave, uncovered, on **HIGH (100%)** for 5 minutes or until soft, stirring after 2½ minutes. Stir in tomatoes and cinnamon. Microwave, uncovered, on **HIGH (100%)** for 3 minutes, stirring after 1½ minutes. Stir in chiles, season to taste with salt, and set aside.

Trim any wax coating from cheese; cut cheese into ¼-inch-thick slices. Overlap slices in a 10-inch microwave-safe pie plate or other shallow 1½-quart baking dish; cheese should cover dish bottom and extend partway up sides.

Microwave, uncovered, on **MEDIUM-HIGH (70–80%)** for 8 minutes, giving dish a half-turn after 4 minutes; cheese should be hot and melted in center. Spread tomato salsa in center of cheese. Microwave, uncovered, on **HIGH (100%)** for 2 minutes or until salsa is hot. Sprinkle shrimp over salsa; microwave, uncovered, on **HIGH (100%)** for 2 minutes or until shrimp are warm.

Scoop cheese, shrimp, and salsa onto warm tortillas; fold to enclose, then eat out of hand. Makes about 6 servings.

Per serving: 637 calories, 39 g protein, 31 g carbohydrates, 40 g total fat, 183 mg cholesterol, 908 mg sodium

SANDWICHES & HEARTY SNACKS

When you need to put together hot sandwiches or satisfying snacks quickly, your microwave oven is just the partner you need. The six recipes featured here are sure to appease midday or evening appetites; serve them at lunchtime, as a light supper, or for a hearty late-night snack.

Our selection includes four sandwiches: hot crab and mushroom, barbecued meatball, chicken and ham, and a Reuben-type treat made with crisp rye crackers. We also offer two tortilla specialties. One's a soft tortilla with a spicy meat filling; the other features puffy tortilla "disks" topped with vegetables and cheese.

CRAB & MUSHROOM SUPREME ON MUFFINS

Preparation time: About 10 minutes
Microwaving time: About 14 minutes

- 1 tablespoon butter or margarine
- ¾ pound mushrooms, sliced
- 1 tablespoon lemon juice
- 2 tablespoons dry sherry
- 1 cup sour cream
- ¾ pound fresh crabmeat or 2 cans (7½ oz. *each*) crabmeat, drained
- 3 tablespoons grated Parmesan cheese
- 4 English muffins, split, toasted, and lightly buttered
- 1 tablespoon minced parsley

Place butter in a 7- by 11-inch microwave-safe baking dish. Microwave, uncovered, on **HIGH (100%)** for about 30 seconds or until butter is melted. Add mushrooms and lemon juice. Microwave, uncovered, on **HIGH (100%)** for 4 minutes, stirring after 2 minutes. Add sherry; microwave, uncovered, on **HIGH (100%)** for 6 minutes or until liquid is reduced by half, stirring after 3 min-

utes. Blend in sour cream, crab, and cheese. Cover; microwave on **HIGH (100%)** for 3 minutes or until heated through, stirring every minute.

Spoon crab mixture evenly over muffin halves; sprinkle with parsley. Eat with knife and fork. Makes 4 servings (2 muffin halves *each*).

Per serving: 408 calories, 26 g protein, 34 g carbohydrates, 19 g total fat, 121 mg cholesterol, 662 mg sodium

OPEN-FACED REUBENS

Preparation time: About 15 minutes
Microwaving time: 3 to 5 minutes

- 2 tablespoons mayonnaise
- 2 teaspoons Dijon mustard
- ½ cup drained canned sauerkraut
- ¼ pound thinly sliced corned beef or pastrami, slivered
- About 5 ounces thinly sliced Swiss cheese
- 12 crisp rye crackers (*each* about 2½ by 4½ inches)
- Thin dill pickle or cornichon slices
- 12 cocktail onions (optional)

In a bowl, stir together mayonnaise and mustard; lightly mix in sauerkraut and corned beef. Set aside.

Place a cheese slice on each cracker. Then top crackers evenly with corned beef mixture; add pickle slices and onions, if desired. Arrange 6 of the sandwiches on a flat microwave-safe plate. Microwave, un-

covered, on **HIGH (100%)** for 1½ to 2½ minutes, giving plate a half-turn after 1 minute. Cheese should be melted; beef mixture should be hot. Repeat to cook remaining 6 sandwiches. Makes 12 servings.

Per serving: 116 calories, 6 g protein, 7 g carbohydrates, 7 g total fat, 21 mg cholesterol, 218 mg sodium

ZESTY BARBECUED MEATBALL SANDWICHES

Preparation time: 15 to 20 minutes
Microwaving time: 8 to 10 minutes

- 1 large egg
- 1 tablespoon Worcestershire
- ¼ teaspoon salt
- ¼ cup *each* fine dry bread crumbs and thinly sliced green onions (including tops)
- 1 pound lean ground beef
- ½ cup prepared barbecue sauce
- 6 frankfurter rolls, split, toasted, and lightly buttered

In a large bowl, beat egg just to blend. Mix in Worcestershire, salt, bread crumbs, and onions. Add beef and mix lightly until well blended. Shape mixture into 1-inch balls. Arrange in a single layer in a 7- by 11-inch microwave-safe baking dish.

Cover and microwave on **HIGH (100%)** for 5 minutes, giving dish a half-turn after 2½ minutes. Spoon off and discard drippings; if necessary, rearrange meatballs to bring any uncooked ones to edges of dish. Drizzle with barbecue sauce.

Microwave, uncovered, on **HIGH (100%)** for 3 to 5 minutes or until meatballs are no longer pink in center; cut to test. Stir meatballs gently to coat with sauce.

To serve, spoon about a sixth of the meatballs and sauce onto each roll (you'll have about 6 meatballs per serving). Makes 6 servings.

Per serving: 317 calories, 19 g protein, 28 g carbohydrates, 14 g total fat, 82 mg cholesterol, 562 mg sodium

FLOPPY DISKS

✳   ✳   ✳   ✳   ✳

Preparation time: About 10 minutes
Microwaving time: 28 to 34 minutes

- 4 flour tortillas (*each* about 8 inches in diameter)
- 1 tablespoon butter or margarine
- 1 medium-size onion, chopped
- ½ pound mushrooms, sliced
- 2 cups (8 oz.) shredded mozzarella cheese
- 1 medium-size firm-ripe tomato, thinly sliced
  Ground nutmeg

Place 1 tortilla on a microwave-safe plate. Microwave, uncovered, on **HIGH (100%)** for 1 minute or until top of tortilla puffs. Turn tortilla over; microwave, uncovered, on **HIGH (100%)** for 1 more minute or until other side puffs. Set aside; tortilla will become crisper as it cools. Repeat with remaining tortillas.

In a 9- by 13-inch microwave-safe baking dish, combine butter, onion, and mushrooms. Cover and microwave on **HIGH (100%)** for 6 minutes, stirring after 3 minutes. Then microwave, uncovered, on **HIGH (100%)** for 8 to 10 minutes or until all liquid has evaporated, stirring every 3 minutes.

Place each tortilla on a micro-wave-safe plate. With a spoon, spread a fourth of the mushroom mixture on each tortilla; spread almost to edges. Scatter cheese evenly over mushroom mixture; top each tortilla with equal portions of tomato. Sprinkle each with nutmeg.

Microwave tortillas, one at a time, uncovered, on **HIGH (100%)** for 1½ to 2½ minutes or until cheese is melted. Makes 4 servings.

Per serving: 278 calories, 15 g protein, 17 g carbohydrates, 18 g total fat, 52 mg cholesterol, 386 mg sodium

CHICKEN MELT SANDWICHES

✳   ✳   ✳   ✳   ✳

Preparation time: About 15 minutes
Microwaving time: 1 minute

- ⅓ cup mayonnaise
- 2 tablespoons Dijon mustard
- ½ teaspoon dry tarragon
  Micro-steamed Chicken Breasts (page 84), shredded
- ¼ cup thinly sliced green onions (including tops)
- 2 tablespoons sweet pickle relish
  Ground red pepper (cayenne)
- 6 croissants (*each* 4 to 5 inches long), split horizontally and toasted
- 6 thin slices cooked ham (1 oz. *each*)
- 6 thin slices Swiss cheese, *each* 3 to 4 inches square (about 4 oz. *total*)

In a bowl, combine mayonnaise, mustard, and tarragon. Add chicken, onions, and pickle relish; mix lightly. Season to taste with red pepper.

Spread bottom halves of croissants with chicken mixture; then top each with a slice of ham and a slice of cheese. Arrange sandwiches spoke fashion on a large microwave-safe plate. Microwave, uncovered, on **HIGH (100%)** for 1 minute or until cheese begins to melt. Cover with croissant tops. Makes 6 servings.

Per serving: 559 calories, 50 g protein, 24 g carbohydrates, 29 g total fat, 151 mg cholesterol, 1,152 mg sodium

TACO JOES

✳   ✳   ✳   ✳   ✳

Preparation time: 5 to 10 minutes
Microwaving time: 16 to 19 minutes

- 1 medium-size onion, minced
- 1 clove garlic, minced or pressed
- 2 teaspoons chili powder
- ½ teaspoon ground cumin
- 1 tablespoon olive oil
- 1 pound lean ground beef or ground turkey
- 1 large can (15 oz.) herb-flavored tomato sauce
- 1 can (4 oz.) diced green chiles
- 1 can (2¼ oz.) sliced ripe olives, drained
- 20 flour tortillas (*each* about 8 inches in diameter)

In a 2½- to 3-quart microwave-safe casserole, combine onion, garlic, chili powder, cumin, and oil. Cover and microwave on **HIGH (100%)** for about 5 minutes or until onion is soft, stirring every 2 minutes.

Crumble beef into onion mixture; stir to blend. Cover and microwave on **HIGH (100%)** for 3 to 5 minutes or until beef is no longer pink on surface, stirring after 1½ minutes.

Mix in tomato sauce, chiles, and olives. Microwave, uncovered, on **HIGH (100%)** for 6 minutes or until hot and bubbly, stirring after 4 minutes. Cover and keep warm.

Divide tortillas into 2 equal stacks. Place each stack in a plastic bag. Microwave, one stack at a time, on **HIGH (100%)** for 1 to 1½ minutes or until tortillas are hot through.

To serve, spoon about ¼ cup of the meat mixture onto each warm tortilla, then roll up and eat out of hand. Makes 20 snacks.

Per snack: 152 calories, 6 g protein, 14 g carbohydrates, 8 g total fat, 17 mg cholesterol, 346 mg sodium

CREAMY PARMESAN FONDUE

Preparation time: About 15 minutes
Microwaving time: About 6 minutes

Mild, mellow cream cheese, melted until smooth, forms the base for this robust fondue. For dippers, offer bell pepper strips, fresh mushrooms, chunks of sausage, and cubes of French bread.

2 large packages (8 oz. *each*) cream cheese
About 2 cups milk

2 cloves garlic, minced or pressed

5 ounces Parmesan cheese, shredded or grated
Freshly ground pepper and ground nutmeg

¼ cup thinly sliced green onions (including tops)

1 pound kielbasa (Polish sausage) or other precooked sausage, cut into l-inch slanting slices and heated

3 medium-size red or green bell peppers, seeded and cut into 1-inch-wide strips

½ pound mushrooms

½ to 1 pound sourdough French bread, cut into 1-inch cubes

Place cream cheese in a 1½-quart microwave-safe casserole or serving dish. Microwave, uncovered, on **HIGH (100%)** for 2 minutes or until very soft. Gradually stir in 2 cups of the milk, blending to make a smooth sauce. Then stir in garlic and Parmesan cheese. Microwave, uncovered, on **HIGH (100%)** for 4 minutes or until Parmesan is melted and sauce is thickened, stirring every minute. Season to taste with pepper and nutmeg. Sprinkle with onions.

To serve, offer sausage, bell pepper strips, whole mushrooms, and bread cubes for dipping; provide fondue forks or long wooden skewers. If fondue cools, reheat it briefly in microwave, adding more milk as needed to maintain a good dipping consistency. Makes about 4 cups fondue (about 6 servings).

Per serving: 854 calories, 35 g protein, 44 g carbohydrates, 60 g total fat, 168 mg cholesterol, 1,698 mg sodium

---

Pictured on page 7

PEA POD & SHRIMP PASTA

Preparation time: About 15 minutes
Microwaving time: About 15 minutes
Standing time: 3 minutes

Fresh linguine, pea pods, and pink shrimp in a creamy Swiss cheese sauce make a quick and satisfying entrée.

1 package (6 oz.) frozen Chinese pea pods

1 package (9 oz.) fresh linguine or fettuccine

1¼ cups regular-strength chicken broth

½ cup dry white wine

1 cup whipping cream

¼ teaspoon dry tarragon

1 pound medium-large raw shrimp (31 to 35 per lb.), shelled and deveined

2 cups (8 oz.) shredded Swiss cheese
Salt and pepper

Microwave unopened package of pea pods on **HIGH (100%)** for 1½ minutes. Let stand for 3 minutes. Open package and pour pea pods into a colander to drain.

Lay pasta in an even layer in a shallow 2- to 2½-quart microwave-safe baking dish. Pour broth, wine, and cream evenly over pasta; sprinkle with tarragon. Cover and microwave on **HIGH (100%)** for 10 minutes, stirring every 3 minutes; pasta should be tender to bite.

Mix in shrimp; microwave, uncovered, on **HIGH (100%)** for 2 minutes. Add cheese and drained pea pods and mix with 2 forks to blend. Season to taste with salt and pepper. Microwave, uncovered, on **HIGH (100%)** for 1 minute or until cheese is melted. Makes about 4 servings.

Per serving: 698 calories, 46 g protein, 43 g carbohydrates, 38 g total fat, 333 mg cholesterol, 632 mg sodium

Elegant yet hearty, these party-perfect Cannelloni (recipe on page 32)
are filled with spinach and sausage, cloaked in a minted tomato sauce, and
generously topped with mild, creamy cheese. Keep accompaniments
simple—just a mixed green salad and a bottle of wine.

Pictured on page 31
CANNELLONI

✳   ✳   ✳   ✳   ✳   ✳   ✳

Preparation time: 15 to 20 minutes
Microwaving time: About 42 minutes
Standing time: 10 minutes

Purchased egg roll wrappers take the place of homemade pasta in this time-saving version of an Italian classic. To make these cannelloni, you wrap egg roll skins around a savory sausage and spinach mixture, then top the rolls with a creamy mint-seasoned tomato sauce and microwave them until the pasta is tender.

  ½   pound mild or hot Italian sausages, casings removed
  5   ounces (half of a 10-oz. package) frozen chopped spinach, thawed and squeezed dry
  1   cup ricotta cheese
  1   large egg yolk
  ½   cup freshly grated Parmesan cheese
  ¼   teaspoon *each* fennel seeds and dry oregano leaves
  ⅛   teaspoon pepper
      Creamy Tomato-Mint Sauce (recipe follows)
  6   egg roll wrappers
  8   ounces teleme or jack cheese, cut into 6 slices

Crumble sausage into an 8- by 12-inch microwave-safe baking dish; cover with a paper towel. Microwave on **HIGH (100%)** for 3 minutes, stirring after 1½ minutes; break up any large chunks of meat with a spoon. With a slotted spoon, transfer sausage to a small bowl. Add spinach, ricotta cheese, egg yolk, Parmesan cheese, fennel seeds, oregano, and pepper. Stir until blended; set aside.

Wipe out baking dish used to cook sausage, then prepare Creamy Tomato-Mint Sauce in baking dish as directed. Scoop out 1 cup of the sauce and set aside.

Mound a sixth of the spinach-sausage filling (about ⅓ cup) in a strip along one long edge of an egg roll wrapper; roll up wrapper to enclose filling. Repeat with remaining filling and wrappers. Arrange cannelloni, seam side down and slightly apart, atop sauce in baking dish; spread reserved 1 cup sauce evenly over cannelloni.

Cover and microwave on **HIGH (100%)** for 12 minutes, giving dish a half-turn after 6 minutes. Then arrange teleme cheese slices evenly over cannelloni; microwave, uncovered, on **HIGH (100%)**

for 5 minutes or until cheese is melted and pasta is tender when pierced. Let stand, uncovered, for 10 minutes. Makes 3 to 6 servings.

Creamy Tomato-Mint Sauce. Place 2 tablespoons **salad oil** in an 8- by 12-inch microwave-safe baking dish. Microwave, uncovered, on **HIGH (100%)** for 1½ minutes. Add l large **onion** (finely chopped) and 1 large clove **garlic** (minced or pressed). Microwave, uncovered, on **HIGH (100%)** for 5 minutes or until onion is soft, stirring after 2½ minutes. Add ¾ cup **regular-strength chicken broth**, ⅓ cup **whipping cream**, 1 tablespoon **dry mint**, 1 teaspoon **dry basil**, and 1 large can (28 oz.) **pear-shaped tomatoes** and their liquid. Cut tomatoes into ½-inch pieces; stir to blend. Microwave, uncovered, on **HIGH (100%)** for 15 minutes, stirring and mashing tomatoes every 5 minutes.

Per serving: 443 calories, 24 g protein, 18 g carbohydrates, 31 g total fat, 98 mg cholesterol, 1,021 mg sodium

✳   **CANNELLONI WITH CHICKEN-PROSCIUTTO FILLING**

Follow directions for **Cannelloni**, but omit sausages, spinach, ricotta cheese, egg yolk, Parmesan cheese, fennel seeds, oregano, and pepper. Instead, prepare this chicken-prosciutto filling:

Coarsely chop 6 ounces thin-sliced **prosciutto** or cooked ham; set aside. Remove bones and skin from 1 pound **chicken breast;** cut meat into ½-inch pieces and set aside.

Place 2 tablespoons **butter** or margarine in a shallow 2½- to 3-quart microwave-safe baking dish. Microwave, uncovered, on **HIGH (100%)** for about 35 seconds or until melted. Add 1 large **onion,** chopped; microwave, uncovered, on **HIGH (100%)** for 5 minutes or until onion is soft, stirring after 2½ minutes. Add chicken. Microwave, uncovered, on **HIGH (100%)** for 3½ to 4 minutes, stirring after 2 minutes. Meat should no longer be pink in center; cut to test.

Transfer chicken mixture to a food processor; add prosciutto. Whirl until meats are coarsely ground. Then mix in 2 large **egg yolks,** l cup **ricotta cheese,** ⅔ cup freshly grated **Parmesan cheese,** and ⅛ to ¼ teaspoon **ground nutmeg.** Season to taste with **salt** and **pepper.**

Per serving: 390 calories, 35 g protein, 10 g carbohydrates, 23 g total fat, 153 mg cholesterol, 1,112 mg sodium

EASY LASAGNE

✳   ✳   ✳   ✳   ✳   ✳   ✳

Preparation time: 10 to 15 minutes
Microwaving time: 37 minutes
Standing time: 15 to 20 minutes

Once upon a time, making lasagne was almost an all-day project. With the advent of the microwave, however, this favorite Italian casserole can be assembled and baked in about an hour.

  4 **cups homemade or purchased marinara sauce**
  1 **teaspoon** *each* **dry oregano leaves and dry basil**
  1 **clove garlic, minced or pressed**
  ½ **cup water**
  8 **ounces dry lasagne**
  ½ **pound lean ground beef**
  3 **cups (12 oz.) shredded Cheddar or jack cheese**
  1 **cup ricotta cheese**
  1 **package (8 oz.) mozzarella cheese, thinly sliced**
  ⅓ **cup freshly grated Parmesan cheese**

In a large bowl, stir together marinara sauce, oregano, basil, and garlic. Pour about a third of the sauce mixture evenly into a 7- by 11-inch microwave-safe baking dish. Stir water into remaining sauce; set aside.

Rinse uncooked lasagne noodles with cold water. Then arrange a third of the uncooked noodles in a single layer atop sauce in baking dish; evenly crumble uncooked beef on top. Sprinkle beef with 1½ cups of the Cheddar cheese; pour a third of the remaining sauce over cheese. Arrange half the remaining lasagne on top; spread with ricotta cheese, sprinkle with remaining 1½ cups Cheddar cheese, and coat with half the remaining sauce. Then layer on remaining lasagne and remaining sauce.

Cover and microwave on **MEDIUM (50%)** for 20 minutes, giving dish a half-turn after 10 minutes. Let stand, covered, for 5 minutes. Then give dish a half-turn; microwave, covered, on **HIGH (100%)** for 15 minutes, giving dish a half-turn every 5 minutes.

Uncover lasagne and arrange mozzarella cheese on top. Sprinkle evenly with Parmesan cheese. Cover and microwave on **HIGH (100%)** for 2 minutes or until cheese is melted. Remove from oven and let stand, covered, for 10 to 15 minutes or until lasagne noodles are tender when pierced. To serve, cut into squares. Makes 6 to 8 servings.

Per serving: 648 calories, 36 g protein, 41 g carbohydrates, 39 g total fat, 114 mg cholesterol, 1,387 mg sodium

CHICKEN NOODLE CASSEROLE

✳   ✳   ✳   ✳   ✳   ✳   ✳

Preparation time: About 10 minutes
Microwaving time: 17 minutes
Standing time: 15 minutes

Here's a new version of an old-fashioned favorite. To make it, you cook the pasta right in the casserole—no need to boil and drain it separately.

  2 **cups regular-strength chicken broth**
  6 **ounces dry wide egg noodles (about 3¼ cups)**
  1 **can (4 oz.) mushroom stems and pieces**
  1 **can (10¾ oz.) condensed reduced-salt cream of chicken soup**
  2 **tablespoons instant minced onion**
  ½ **teaspoon dry rosemary**
  ¼ **teaspoon pepper**
  2 **cups bite-size pieces cooked chicken or 1 large can (12½ oz.) chunk-style tuna, drained**
  1 **cup frozen peas, thawed**
  ¼ **cup toasted sliced almonds**

Pour broth into a 3-quart microwave-safe casserole. Cover and microwave on **HIGH (100%)** for 3 minutes or until broth comes to a boil. Add noodles, pressing them down into broth. Cover and microwave on **HIGH (100%)** for 8 minutes, stirring after 4 minutes. Remove casserole from oven; let stand, covered, for 5 minutes.

Stir in undrained mushrooms, soup, onion, rosemary, pepper, and chicken; stir to blend. Cover and microwave on **HIGH (100%)** for 5 minutes, stirring after 2½ minutes. Mix in peas. Cover and microwave on **HIGH (100%)** for 1 minute. Remove casserole from oven and let stand, covered, for 10 minutes or until noodles are tender when pierced. Garnish with almonds. Makes about 4 servings.

Per serving: 477 calories, 33 g protein, 47 g carbohydrates, 17 g total fat, 102 mg cholesterol, 1,090 mg sodium

Here's a lovely dinner for two: fresh asparagus, buttered red potatoes, and Steak with Mustard-Caper Sauce (recipe on page 36). The tender cube steaks are sizzled briefly in a microwave browning dish, then topped with a piquant blend of butter, sherry, Dijon mustard, and capers.

Meats

If you've been reluctant to try cooking meats in the microwave, this chapter will help change your mind. We've found that certain cuts of meat are well suited to microwave cooking. Ground beef, pork, and lamb make tempting burgers, meatballs, and casseroles; spareribs, cooked at a reduced power, turn out juicy and tender. You can even flip a steak in a browning dish and have it ready to serve, complete with sauce, in about 10 minutes. To help you develop your own recipes, we've included a meat cooking chart.

Pictured on page 34

STEAK WITH MUSTARD-CAPER SAUCE

✻   ✻   ✻   ✻   ✻   ✻   ✻

Preparation time: About 2 minutes
Microwaving time: About 7 minutes
Standing time: 2 minutes

The lean, boneless steaks labeled "cube steaks" or "minute steaks" in the meat market are actually beef round steak—first cut into individual portions, then run through a mechanical tenderizer. Briefly cooked, then sauced with mustard and sherry, these steaks make a tasty entrée in under 10 minutes.

   2 cube steaks (about 6 oz. *each*)
   4 teaspoons prepared steak sauce
   2 tablespoons dry sherry
   2 teaspoons Dijon mustard
   ¼ teaspoon Worcestershire
   1 tablespoon capers, drained
   2 tablespoons butter or margarine
      Watercress sprigs

Brush each side of each steak with 1 teaspoon of the steak sauce. Set steaks aside.

Preheat a 2- to 2½-quart or 10-inch square microwave browning dish on **HIGH (100%)** for 4½ minutes. Meanwhile, stir together sherry, mustard, Worcestershire, and capers; set aside.

Using oven mitts, carefully remove browning dish to a heatproof surface. Add steaks and wait until sizzling stops. Then turn steaks over and microwave, uncovered, on **HIGH (100%)** for 45 seconds. Transfer steaks to a platter, cover loosely, and let stand for 2 minutes.

Meanwhile, add butter to browning dish and microwave, uncovered, on **HIGH (100%)** for 25 to 30 seconds or until melted. Stir in sherry mixture and microwave, uncovered, on **HIGH (100%)** for 45 seconds or until hot through. Pour sauce over steaks and garnish with watercress. Makes 2 servings.

Per serving: 534 calories, 33 g protein, 5 g carbohydrates, 42 g total fat, 143 mg cholesterol, 656 mg sodium

ORIENTAL BEEF

✻   ✻   ✻   ✻   ✻   ✻   ✻

Preparation time: 15 to 20 minutes
Microwaving time: 9 to 11 minutes
Standing time: 1 minute

Here's a tasty filling for pocket bread rounds—tender beef or pork strips, crisp bean sprouts, and green onions in a gingery Oriental-style sauce.

   ¼ cup water
   1 tablespoon cornstarch
   2 tablespoons *each* soy sauce and
      dry sherry
   1 teaspoon sugar
   ¾ pound lean boneless beef chuck or
      pork shoulder
   2 cloves garlic, minced or pressed
   2 teaspoons minced fresh ginger
      or 1 teaspoon ground ginger
   ¼ teaspoon pepper
   ½ pound bean sprouts
   ⅓ cup sliced green onions (including tops)
   3 pocket breads, cut into halves

In a 2-cup glass measure, stir together water, cornstarch, soy, sherry, and sugar; set aside.

Trim and discard excess fat from meat. Then cut meat into very thin 1- by 3-inch strips, place in a 2½- to 3-quart microwave-safe casserole, and mix in garlic, ginger, and pepper. Cover and microwave on **HIGH (100%)** for 3 to 4 minutes or until meat is no longer pink, stirring after 2 minutes.

Spoon off liquid from meat mixture and add to cornstarch mixture in glass measure; then microwave, uncovered, on **HIGH (100%)** for 3 minutes or until sauce is bubbly, thickened, and clear, stirring every minute. Stir sauce into meat mixture, then stir in bean sprouts and onions. Microwave, uncovered, on **HIGH (100%)** for 2 to 3 minutes or until hot through, stirring after 1½ minutes. Cover and let stand for 1 minute.

Place pocket bread halves in a plastic bag; microwave on **HIGH (100%)** for 30 to 45 seconds or until hot through.

Spoon meat mixture into a warm serving bowl. To serve, spoon into warm pocket bread halves. Makes 3 servings (2 filled bread halves *each*).

Per serving: 421 calories, 31 g protein, 49 g carbohydrates, 11 g total fat, 74 mg cholesterol, 1,143 mg sodium

✳ MEAT COOKING CHART ✳

CAUTION: To prevent overcooking, use shortest cooking time. Allow food to stand for recommended time. On standing, internal temperature of meat will rise 10° to 15°F. If necessary, continue to microwave in 1-minute increments. To cover meat for cooking, you may use heavy-duty plastic wrap, the container lid, or (to cover loosely) wax paper.

MEAT	PREPARATION	COOKING TIME (CT) STANDING TIME (ST)
Beef roast, boneless, round in shape (sirloin tip, rolled rib, cross rib) (3½–4 lbs.)	Trim excess fat from beef. Place beef, fat side down, on a microwave-safe rack in a 7- by 11-inch microwave-safe baking dish. Cover loosely.	**CT:** 9–11 minutes per lb. for rare 10–13 minutes per lb. for medium Determine total cooking time. Microwave on **HIGH (100%)** for 5 minutes, then on **MEDIUM (50%)** for remaining time, giving dish ¼ turn every 10 minutes. Turn roast over halfway through cooking and baste with juices. Meat thermometer or probe inserted in center of roast should register 125°F for rare, 135°F for medium. **ST:** 10–15 minutes, loosely covered with foil.
Ground beef patties (¼ lb. *each*)	Season to taste with salt, pepper, Worcestershire, and finely chopped onion. Shape into patties about ¾ inch thick. If desired, brush patties with a mixture of 2 tablespoons *each* water and bottled brown gravy sauce.	**CT:** Heat a microwave browning griddle or dish on **HIGH (100%)** for 4½ minutes. Using oven mitts, carefully remove dish to a heatproof surface. Add patties to dish; let stand for 1 minute, then turn over. Then microwave, uncovered, on **HIGH (100%)** for times specified below (for medium doneness). 1 patty About 2 minutes 3 patties About 4 minutes 2 patties 2–3 minutes 4 patties About 4 minutes **ST:** 1 minute, uncovered.
Pork loin roast, boneless (3–3½ lbs.)	Trim excess fat from pork. Place pork, fat side down, on a microwave-safe rack in a 7- by 11-inch microwave-safe baking dish.	**CT:** 14–16 minutes per lb. Microwave, uncovered, on **MEDIUM-HIGH (70–80%)**, giving dish ½ turn every 10 minutes. Turn roast over halfway through cooking and baste with juices. Meat thermometer or probe inserted in thickest part should register 150°–155°F. **ST:** 10–15 minutes, loosely covered with foil.
Spareribs, country-style (3 lbs.)	Trim excess fat from ribs. Arrange ribs in a 7- by 11-inch microwave-safe baking dish, with meaty portions to outside of dish. Pour in ¼ cup water. Cover.	**CT:** 18–20 minutes per lb. Determine total cooking time. Microwave, covered, on **HIGH (100%)** for 10 minutes. Pour off juices and turn ribs over. Microwave on **MEDIUM (50%)** for remaining time, discarding accumulated juices and bringing cooked portion to inside of dish halfway through cooking. If desired, uncover and baste with barbecue sauce for last 10 minutes. **ST:** 5 minutes, covered (uncovered, if basted). Meat in thickest part should no longer be pink; cut to test.
Spareribs, one medium-size side (2½–3 lbs.)	Trim excess fat from ribs. Cut ribs into 2-rib pieces. Arrange ribs in a 9- by 13-inch microwave-safe baking dish, with meaty portions to outside of dish. Thinner portions may overlap. Pour in ¼ cup water. Cover.	**CT:** 13–16 minutes per lb. Determine total cooking time. Microwave on **HIGH (100%)** for 7 minutes. Pour off liquid and turn ribs over. Microwave on **MEDIUM (50%)** for remaining time, discarding accumulated juices and bringing cooked portion to inside of dish halfway through cooking. If desired, uncover and baste with barbecue sauce for last 10 minutes. **ST:** 5 minutes, covered (uncovered, if basted). Meat in thickest part should no longer be pink; cut to test.
Leg of veal, boned and tied (4 lbs.)	If desired, rub veal with garlic powder, paprika, and pepper. Place veal, fat side down, on a microwave-safe rack in a 7- by 11-inch microwave-safe baking dish. Cover loosely.	**CT:** 10 minutes per lb. Microwave on **HIGH (100%)**, giving dish ¼ turn every 10 minutes. Turn roast over halfway through cooking and baste with juices. Meat thermometer or probe inserted in thickest part should register 155°F. **ST:** 10 minutes, loosely covered with foil.

Pictured on facing page

PIZZA-TOPPED MEAT LOAF

✳   ✳   ✳   ✳   ✳   ✳   ✳   ✳

Preparation time: 10 to 15 minutes
Microwaving time: 18 to 20 minutes
Standing time: 3 to 5 minutes

Baked in a round or rectangular dish, this moist, herb-seasoned meat loaf is embellished with favorite pizza toppings.

  2 pounds lean ground beef
  ½ cup oat bran
  2 large eggs
  1 small onion, finely chopped
  1 can (15 oz.) pizza sauce
  ¾ teaspoon *each* dry oregano leaves and dry basil
  ½ teaspoon *each* garlic salt and dry thyme leaves
  ¼ teaspoon pepper
  1 can (2¼ oz.) sliced ripe olives, drained
  4 to 6 large mushrooms, thinly sliced
  1 cup (4 oz.) shredded mozzarella cheese
  ½ cup grated Parmesan cheese

In a large bowl, combine beef, oat bran, eggs, onion, ½ cup of the pizza sauce, oregano, basil, garlic salt, thyme, and pepper. Mix well, then pat into a round 2-quart or 7- by 11-inch microwave-safe baking dish.

Microwave, uncovered, on **HIGH (100%)** for 12 minutes, giving dish a half-turn every 4 minutes. Drain excess drippings from dish; spread remaining pizza sauce over top of meat loaf. Distribute olives and mushrooms over sauce, then evenly sprinkle with mozzarella and Parmesan cheeses. Microwave, uncovered, on **HIGH (100%)** for 6 to 8 minutes or until meat loaf is no longer pink in center; cut to test.

Let stand, covered, for 3 to 5 minutes. To serve, cut into wedges or squares. Makes 6 to 8 servings.

Per serving: 427 calories, 33 g protein, 9 g carbohydrates, 28 g total fat, 153 mg cholesterol, 692 mg sodium

SPANISH BEEF & BARLEY

✳   ✳   ✳   ✳   ✳   ✳   ✳

Preparation time: 15 to 20 minutes
Microwaving time: 27 to 32 minutes
Standing time: 3 to 5 minutes

Spoon this spicy blend of tomatoes, ground beef, and barley into pocket bread halves for a satisfying meal. (If you're counting calories, you might substitute crisp butter lettuce leaves for the bread.)

  1 can (14½ oz.) tomatoes
  2 tablespoons chili powder
  1 teaspoon *each* ground cumin and dry oregano leaves
  1 cup pearl barley
  1½ cups water
  1 pound lean ground beef
  1 large onion, finely chopped
  ½ cup diced green bell pepper
  1 clove garlic, minced or pressed
  ¾ cup raisins
     Salt and pepper
  6 to 8 pocket breads, cut into halves
     Plain yogurt

Drain liquid from tomatoes into a 2-quart microwave-safe baking dish; set tomatoes aside. To tomato liquid, add chili powder, cumin, oregano, barley, and water; stir well. Cover and microwave on **HIGH (100%)** for 15 minutes, giving dish a half-turn every 5 minutes. Then set aside, covered, until liquid has been absorbed (about 10 minutes).

Meanwhile, crumble beef into a 2½- to 3-quart microwave-safe casserole; stir in onion, bell pepper, and garlic. Microwave, uncovered, on **HIGH (100%)** for 10 to 12 minutes or until beef is no longer pink, stirring after 5 minutes. Stir in raisins and drained tomatoes (break up with a spoon). Taste barley; if it is not tender to bite, microwave on **HIGH (100%)** for 2 to 3 more minutes. Stir barley mixture into meat mixture; season to taste with salt and pepper. Let stand, covered, for 3 to 5 minutes.

Place pocket bread halves in a plastic bag; microwave on **HIGH (100%)** for about 1½ minutes or until hot through. To serve, spoon beef mixture into pocket bread; top each serving with yogurt. Makes 6 to 8 servings (2 filled bread halves *each*).

Per serving: 520 calories, 22 g protein, 76 g carbohydrates, 15 g total fat, 49 mg cholesterol, 531 mg sodium

*Pizza lovers take note—now there's a meat loaf just for you!
Layered on our Pizza-topped Meat Loaf (recipe on facing page) are
herbed tomato sauce, olives, mushrooms, and two cheeses. To carry out the
Italian theme, garnish the loaf with red and green bell pepper rings.*

SPEEDY PICADILLO

✳ ✳ ✳ ✳ ✳ ✳ ✳

Preparation time: 15 to 20 minutes
Microwaving time: 19 to 23 minutes
Standing time: 1 to 2 minutes

Sweet spices, raisins, and crunchy almonds add interest to a taco-style filling you wrap up in soft flour tortillas. Alongside, offer a platter of sliced tomatoes and cucumbers and a pitcher of beer.

½ cup slivered blanched almonds
1 pound lean ground beef
1 small onion, chopped
2 cloves garlic, minced or pressed
½ cup *each* raisins and catsup
1 teaspoon *each* ground cinnamon and red wine vinegar
¼ teaspoon ground cloves
3 tablespoons hot water
Salt and pepper
12 flour tortillas (*each* about 8 inches in diameter)
2 to 2½ cups shredded iceberg lettuce
About 1½ cups (6 oz.) shredded Cheddar cheese

Spread almonds in a 9- or 10-inch square microwave-safe baking dish. Microwave, uncovered, on **HIGH (100%)** for 6 to 8 minutes or until almonds are golden, stirring every 2 minutes. Pour almonds out of dish and set aside.

Crumble beef into dish. Microwave, uncovered, on **HIGH (100%)** for 4 minutes, stirring after 2 minutes. Stir in onion and garlic; microwave, uncovered, on **HIGH (100%)** for about 5 minutes or until onion is soft, stirring after 2½ minutes. Add raisins, catsup, cinnamon, vinegar, cloves, water, and almonds. Microwave, uncovered, on **HIGH (100%)** for 3 to 4 minutes or until hot through, stirring after 2 minutes. Season to taste with salt and pepper. Cover and let stand for 1 to 2 minutes.

Meanwhile, place tortillas in a plastic bag (or, if using a package of 12 tortillas, poke 3 or 4 holes in top of package). Microwave on **HIGH (100%)** for 1 to 1½ minutes or until tortillas are hot through.

Spoon hot meat filling down center of each tortilla; top with lettuce and cheese, then roll up and eat out of hand. Makes 6 servings (2 tacos *each*).

Per serving: 678 calories, 30 g protein, 68 g carbohydrates, 32 g total fat, 87 mg cholesterol, 888 mg sodium

QUICK BARBECUED BEEF

✳ ✳ ✳ ✳ ✳ ✳ ✳

Preparation time: 5 to 10 minutes
Microwaving time: 13 to 15 minutes
Standing time: 3 to 5 minutes

Feed six hungry people in a hurry with these Sloppy Joe–style sandwiches, easily rustled up from ingredients you probably already have on hand. Any leftovers can be frozen, then microwaved for another meal.

1 pound lean ground beef
1 small onion, finely chopped
1 clove garlic, minced or pressed
1 can (6 oz.) tomato paste
½ cup *each* hot water and sweet pickle relish
1 teaspoon Worcestershire
Salt and pepper
3 English muffins

Preheat a 2- to 2½-quart or 10-inch square microwave browning dish on **HIGH (100%)** for 4½ minutes. Using oven mitts, carefully remove dish to a heatproof surface. Crumble in beef and stir until sizzling stops; then cover and microwave on **HIGH (100%)** for 2 minutes. Break up beef, then stir in onion and garlic.

Cover and microwave on **HIGH (100%)** for 4 minutes, stirring after 2 minutes. Drain off and discard excess fat. Stir in tomato paste, water, pickle relish, and Worcestershire. Season to taste with salt and pepper. Cover and microwave on **HIGH (100%)** for 2 to 4 minutes or until hot through, stirring every 2 minutes. Let stand, covered, for 3 to 5 minutes. Meanwhile, split and toast English muffins.

To serve, spoon hot beef mixture evenly over muffin halves. Makes 6 servings.

Per serving: 271 calories, 17 g protein, 26 g carbohydrates, 11 g total fat, 44 mg cholesterol, 555 mg sodium

BEEF & MUSHROOM BAKE

Preparation time: 15 to 20 minutes
Microwaving time: 17 to 20 minutes
Standing time: 5 minutes

A bubbly cheese topping crowns this casserole of ground beef, spinach, and mushrooms. Accompany it with a crisp green salad and crusty bread.

- 1 pound lean ground beef
- 2 tablespoons butter or margarine
- ½ pound mushrooms, sliced
- 1 medium-size onion, chopped
- 2 packages (10 oz. *each*) frozen chopped spinach, thawed and squeezed dry
- 1 cup sour cream
- ½ teaspoon *each* dry oregano leaves, dry basil, and dry thyme leaves
- ¼ teaspoon pepper
- ⅛ teaspoon ground nutmeg
- 1 cup (4 oz.) shredded sharp Cheddar cheese
- 1 cup (about 5 oz.) grated Parmesan cheese

Crumble beef into a 7- by 11-inch microwave-safe baking dish. Microwave, uncovered, on **HIGH (100%)** for 5 to 7 minutes or until meat is no longer pink; drain off and discard drippings, then remove meat from dish and set aside.

Place butter in same dish; microwave, uncovered, on **HIGH (100%)** for about 35 seconds or until melted. Stir in mushrooms and onion, cover, and microwave on **HIGH (100%)** for 4 minutes, stirring after 2 minutes. Stir in beef, spinach, sour cream, oregano, basil, thyme, pepper, nutmeg, ½ cup of the Cheddar cheese, and ½ cup of the Parmesan cheese. Sprinkle remaining ½ cup of each cheese over top. Microwave, uncovered, on **HIGH (100%)** for 7 to 8 minutes or until hot throughout, giving dish a half-turn after 4 minutes. Let stand, covered, for 5 minutes. Makes 6 servings.

Per serving: 443 calories, 29 g protein, 10 g carbohydrates, 33 g total fat, 101 mg cholesterol, 535 mg sodium

PORK CHOPS OLÉ

Preparation time: About 15 minutes
Microwaving time: 27 to 29 minutes
Standing time: 5 minutes

Many Mexican dishes are attractive candidates for microwave cooking: they emerge from the microwave looking just as lively and colorful as when cooked conventionally, but in a fraction of the time.

- 4 shoulder pork chops (2 to 2½ lbs. *total*), *each* ½ to ¾ inch thick
- 1 tablespoon butter or margarine
- 1 medium-size onion, finely chopped
- 1 clove garlic, minced or pressed
- 2 cups cooked white or brown rice
- ½ cup *each* dried currants and chopped green bell pepper
- 1 can (2¼ oz.) sliced ripe olives, drained
- 1 can (8 oz.) tomato sauce
- 2 teaspoons chili powder
- 1 teaspoon sugar
- ½ teaspoon *each* ground cumin and dry oregano leaves
  Fresh cilantro (coriander) sprigs

Trim excess fat from chops, then arrange chops in a 7- by 11-inch microwave-safe baking dish. Cover and microwave on **HIGH (100%)** for 10 minutes; give dish a half-turn several times and turn chops over after 5 minutes. Lift out chops and set aside. Drain off drippings into a 2-cup glass measure; set aside.

Place butter, onion, and garlic in baking dish; microwave, uncovered, on **HIGH (100%)** for 5 minutes, stirring after 2½ minutes. Stir in rice, currants, bell pepper, and olives.

Skim and discard fat from drippings; stir in tomato sauce, chili powder, sugar, cumin, and oregano. Stir ⅓ cup of the sauce mixture into rice mixture; arrange chops on top of rice mixture, then spoon remaining sauce over top. Cover and microwave on **MEDIUM-HIGH (70–80%)** for 12 to 14 minutes, giving dish a half-turn every 4 minutes. Let stand, covered, for 5 minutes. Meat near bone should no longer be pink; cut to test. Garnish with cilantro. Makes 4 servings.

Per serving: 542 calories, 40 g protein, 47 g carbohydrates, 21 g total fat, 132 mg cholesterol, 649 mg sodium

A hot and hearty meal for a chilly day, Polish Sausage with Cabbage (recipe on facing page) features juicy kielbasa on a bed of dill-seasoned cabbage and apples. Serve with rye bread and your favorite whole-grain mustard.

Pictured on facing page

POLISH SAUSAGE WITH CABBAGE

✳   ✳   ✳   ✳   ✳   ✳   ✳

Preparation time: About 10 minutes
Microwaving time: 14 to 16 minutes
Standing time: 5 minutes

Spicy sausages and sweet chunks of apple lend pleasing flavor to shredded cabbage in this one-dish meal.

>   2   **tablespoons butter or margarine**
>   ½   **cup thinly sliced green onions**
>   **(including tops)**
>   1   **small head green cabbage (about**
>   **1¼ lbs.), cored and coarsely chopped**
>   1   **small Red Delicious apple, cored**
>   **and diced**
>   ½   **teaspoon dry dill weed**
>   **Salt and pepper**
>   1   **pound kielbasa (Polish sausage)**
>   **Spicy brown mustard**

Place butter in a 3-quart microwave-safe casserole. Microwave, uncovered, on **HIGH (100%)** for about 35 seconds or until melted. Add onions and micro-wave, uncovered, on **HIGH (100%)** for 1½ minutes. Stir in cabbage, apple, and dill weed; then season to taste with salt and pepper.

Cut ¼-inch-deep slashes in sausages at about 1-inch intervals; place sausages atop cabbage mixture. Cover and microwave on **HIGH (100%)** for 12 to 14 minutes or until cabbage is tender-crisp to bite; stir cabbage mixture and turn sausages over every 4 to 5 minutes. Let stand, covered, for 5 minutes. Offer mustard at the table to add to individual servings. Makes 4 servings.

Per serving: 473 calories, 18 g protein, 14 g carbohydrates, 39 g total fat, 95 mg cholesterol, 1,079 mg sodium

SPAGHETTI SQUASH SUPPER

✳   ✳   ✳   ✳   ✳   ✳   ✳

Preparation time: About 15 minutes
Microwaving time: 28 to 31 minutes
Standing time: 3 to 5 minutes

With its crisp texture and nutlike flavor, spaghetti squash is the ideal foundation for an aromatic topping of Italian sausage in herbed tomato sauce.

>   1   **spaghetti squash (about 3 lbs.)**
>   1   **pound mild Italian sausages**
>   1   **medium-size onion, finely chopped**
>   ¼   **pound mushrooms, sliced**
>   ½   **teaspoon *each* dry basil and dry oregano**
>   **leaves**
>   1   **jar (15 oz.) spaghetti sauce**
>   **Chopped parsley**
>   **Freshly grated Parmesan cheese**

Rinse squash and pat dry. With a sharp fork, pierce squash shell in 10 to 12 places. Place squash on a paper towel on floor of microwave; then microwave on **HIGH (100%)** for 12 minutes, turning squash over every 4 minutes. Loosely cover squash and set aside.

Remove sausage casings and crumble meat into a 2-quart microwave-safe casserole. Cover with a paper towel; then microwave on **HIGH (100%)** for 5 minutes, stirring after 2½ minutes. Drain off and discard drippings; stir in onion and mushrooms.

Cover and microwave on **HIGH (100%)** for 6 minutes, stirring after 3 minutes. Stir basil and oregano into spaghetti sauce, then stir sauce into sausage mixture. Microwave, uncovered, on **HIGH (100%)** for 5 minutes or until steaming, stirring after 3 minutes. Let stand, covered, for 3 to 5 minutes.

Press squash shell; if shell does not give to pressure, microwave squash on **HIGH (100%)** for 2 to 3 more minutes.

To serve, split squash in half lengthwise; scoop out and discard seeds. Pull strands free with a fork. Evenly top with sausage sauce and sprinkle with parsley. Lift strands and sauce from shell halves to individual plates. Pass cheese at the table to sprinkle over individual servings. Makes 4 to 6 servings.

Per serving: 383 calories, 17 g protein, 30 g carbohydrates, 22 g total fat, 52 mg cholesterol, 1,068 mg sodium

LEMONY COUNTRY-STYLE RIBS

Preparation time: About 10 minutes
Microwaving time: About 1 hour
Standing time: 5 to 10 minutes

A tantalizing aroma will fill the air when you cook these meaty ribs. To take full advantage of the flavorful sauce, serve the ribs with hot cooked rice.

- 1 large onion, finely chopped
- 1 lemon, thinly sliced
- 3 pounds country-style spareribs
- ⅓ cup honey
- 2 tablespoons soy sauce
- ¼ cup lemon juice
- 1 teaspoon minced fresh ginger
- 1 clove garlic, minced or pressed
- 1 tablespoon *each* cornstarch and water
- ¼ teaspoon pepper

Evenly distribute onion in a 10-inch square microwave-safe baking dish with a lid; top onion evenly with lemon slices. Trim and discard excess fat from ribs, then arrange ribs on top of lemon slices. Cover and microwave on **HIGH (100%)** for 10 minutes.

Meanwhile, combine honey, soy, lemon juice, ginger, and garlic. Pour honey mixture over partially cooked ribs. Cover and microwave on **MEDIUM (50%)** for 45 minutes or until spareribs are tender when pierced; turn and reposition ribs every 10 minutes.

Lift ribs to a plate; cover and let stand for 5 to 10 minutes. Meanwhile, prepare sauce: Discard lemon slices, then skim and discard fat from drippings. Combine cornstarch and water; stir into drippings along with pepper. Microwave, uncovered, on **HIGH (100%)** for 4 to 5 minutes or until thickened, stirring every 2 minutes. Return ribs and any juices to sauce, then serve. Makes 4 servings.

Per serving: 648 calories, 40 g protein, 33 g carbohydrates, 40 g total fat, 161 mg cholesterol, 644 mg sodium

ORANGE-GLAZED PORK RIBS

Preparation time: 10 minutes
Microwaving time: 30 to 32 minutes
Standing time: 5 minutes

Barbecued ribs in half an hour? It's easy when you use the microwave. These tender pork ribs are glazed in a sweet orange sauce nipped with mustard and horseradish.

- ¼ cup frozen concentrated orange juice, thawed
- 3 tablespoons tomato-based chili sauce or catsup
- 2 tablespoons lemon juice
- 1 tablespoon firmly packed brown sugar
- 1½ teaspoons Worcestershire
- 1 teaspoon prepared mustard
- ¼ to ½ teaspoon prepared horseradish
- 2½ to 3 pounds pork baby back ribs

In a 1-cup glass measure, stir together orange juice, chili sauce, lemon juice, sugar, Worcestershire, mustard, and horseradish. Microwave, uncovered, on **HIGH (100%)** for 2 minutes; set aside.

Trim and discard excess fat from ribs. Place ribs in a 7- by 11-inch microwave-safe baking dish. Cover and microwave on **HIGH (100%)** for 10 minutes. Drain off and discard accumulated juices.

Turn ribs over; move uncooked center ribs to outside of dish and bring cooked ribs to inside. Pour sauce over ribs. Cover and microwave on **MEDIUM (50%)** for 10 minutes. Uncover. Turn ribs over, baste, and microwave, uncovered, on **MEDIUM (50%)** for 8 to 10 minutes, basting every 3 to 4 minutes. Meat near bone should no longer be pink; cut to test. Let stand, covered, for 5 minutes. Makes 3 servings.

Per serving: 723 calories, 48 g protein, 19 g carbohydrates, 49 g total fat, 196 mg cholesterol, 433 mg sodium

SATISFYING
WHOLE-MEAL
SALADS

When the weather is hot, when you feel like eating light, or when you just want a change of pace, these fresh, hearty salads fill the bill perfectly.

HOT CHICKEN SALAD IN TOMATO CUPS

Pictured on page 95

Preparation time: 35 minutes
Microwaving time: About 6 minutes
Standing time: 1 minute

1 whole chicken breast (about 1 lb.), skinned, boned, and split
2 large tomatoes, peeled
   Lettuce leaves
⅓ cup *each* chopped green onions (including tops) and celery
1 jar (2 oz.) sliced pimentos, drained
1 jar (6 oz.) marinated artichoke hearts, drained and chopped
½ cup shredded Cheddar cheese
3 tablespoons mayonnaise
   Salt and pepper
   Chopped parsley

Microwave chicken as directed in chart on page 77. Drain off and discard juices; set chicken aside.

Cut cores out of tomatoes. Then, without cutting all the way through, cut each tomato into 6 to 8 wedges. Line 2 salad plates with lettuce and place a tomato on each. Spread tomatoes open; set aside.

In a 2-quart microwave-safe bowl, combine onions, celery, pimentos (reserve a few slices for garnish), artichokes, cheese, and mayonnaise. Cut chicken into bite-size pieces; add to bowl and stir just to blend. Season to taste with salt and pepper. Cover and microwave on **MEDIUM (50%)** for 3 minutes or until heated through, stirring after 1½ minutes. Mound chicken mixture in tomato cups; garnish with pimento slices and parsley. Makes 2 servings.

Per serving: 581 calories, 46 g protein, 21 g carbohydrates, 37 g total fat, 135 mg cholesterol, 855 mg sodium

ZAPPED TACO SALAD

Preparation time: About 20 minutes
Microwaving time: 20 to 22 minutes

1 pound lean ground beef
1 medium-size onion, chopped
1 can (about 15 oz.) kidney beans, drained
1 can (about 1 lb.) stewed tomatoes
1 can (4 oz.) diced green chiles
2 tablespoons chili powder
1 medium-size head iceberg lettuce, shredded
2 tomatoes, cut into wedges
   About 5 cups corn chips
1 cup (4 oz.) shredded sharp Cheddar cheese

Crumble beef into a 9- by 13-inch microwave-safe baking dish; add onion. Cover and microwave on **HIGH (100%)** for 5 minutes, stirring after 3 minutes. Uncover and microwave on **HIGH (100%)** for 5 to 7 minutes or until meat is no longer pink, stirring every 3 minutes. Discard drippings.

Stir beans, tomatoes, chiles, and chili powder into meat mixture. Cover and microwave on **HIGH (100%)** for 10 minutes or until bubbly; stir every 2 to 3 minutes.

Mound lettuce on 5 individual plates. Arrange tomato wedges and corn chips around lettuce. Spoon hot meat mixture onto lettuce; top with cheese. Makes 5 servings.

Per serving: 658 calories, 32 g protein, 53 g carbohydrates, 38 g total fat, 78 mg cholesterol, 1,208 mg sodium

POACHED FISH & SPINACH SALAD

Preparation time: 15 to 20 minutes
Microwaving time: 3 to 4 minutes
Standing time: 3 minutes
Chilling time: At least 2 hours

1 pound skinless white-fleshed fish fillets, such as sole or snapper (each ½ to ¾ inch thick)
   Curry Dressing (recipe follows)
4 to 5 cups lightly packed torn spinach leaves
1 hard-cooked egg, thinly sliced
⅓ cup unsalted dry-roasted cashews, coarsely chopped

Microwave unseasoned fish as directed in chart on page 53. Let cool, then cover and refrigerate for at least 2 hours or up to 8 hours. Also prepare dressing and refrigerate.

Gently break fish into bite-size pieces; discard any bones. Arrange spinach on individual plates. Mound fish in center; spoon a little dressing over all. Garnish salad with egg and cashews. Pass remaining dressing at the table. Makes 3 servings.

Curry Dressing. Mix ½ cup **plain yogurt**; 1 teaspoon *each* **Dijon mustard, curry powder, lemon juice,** and **sugar;** and ¼ teaspoon *each* **ground cumin** and **ground turmeric.**

Per serving: 314 calories, 40 g protein, 13 g carbohydrates, 12 g total fat, 129 mg cholesterol, 209 mg sodium

PORK BURGERS

✳   ✳   ✳   ✳   ✳   ✳   ✳

Preparation time: 10 minutes
Microwaving time: About 10 minutes
Standing time: 3 minutes

Cooked in a browning dish, these moist pork patties look pan-fried. Serve them in hamburger buns; or top the patties with pineapple rings and serve them open-faced on English muffin halves.

- ½ **pound lean ground pork**
- 1 **large egg**
- 1 **clove garlic, minced or pressed**
- ⅓ **cup *each* finely chopped onion and chopped green bell pepper**
- ½ **teaspoon dry oregano leaves**
- ¼ **teaspoon *each* salt, pepper, and ground cumin**
- 2 **tablespoons oat bran or fine dry bread crumbs**
- 2 **hamburger buns**
- 4 **thin tomato slices**
- 2 **to 4 lettuce leaves**

In a bowl, combine pork, egg, garlic, onion, bell pepper, oregano, salt, pepper, cumin, and oat bran. Blend well, then shape mixture into 2 patties, each about ½ inch thick.

Preheat a 2- to 2½-quart or 10-inch square microwave browning dish on **HIGH (100%)** for 4½ minutes. Using oven mitts, carefully remove dish to a heatproof surface. Immediately place patties in dish. Wait until sizzling stops, then cover and microwave on **HIGH (100%)** for 3 minutes. Turn patties over and microwave, uncovered, on **HIGH (100%)** for 2 minutes or until no longer pink in center; cut to test. Cover and let patties stand for 3 minutes. Meanwhile, split and toast hamburger buns.

To serve, place patties on bottom halves of buns and top each with 2 tomato slices and 1 or 2 lettuce leaves. Cover with bun tops. Makes 2 servings.

Per serving: 414 calories, 29 g protein, 29 g carbohydrates, 20 g total fat, 192 mg cholesterol, 569 mg sodium

---

Pictured on facing page

MINTED LAMB MEATBALLS WITH LEMON SAUCE

✳   ✳   ✳   ✳   ✳   ✳   ✳

Preparation time: 15 minutes
Microwaving time: 8 minutes
Standing time: 4 minutes

These tender meatballs, pungent with mint and garlic, are spooned over hot rice and topped with a mildly tart lemon sauce.

- ½ **cup regular-strength chicken broth**
- 1 **tablespoon lemon juice**
- 1½ **teaspoons cornstarch**
- 1 **large egg**
- 2 **teaspoons dry mint**
- 1 **large clove garlic, minced or pressed**
- 1 **tablespoon all-purpose flour**
- ¼ **teaspoon *each* salt and pepper**
- ¾ **pound lean ground lamb**
- 2 **tablespoons minced green onion (including top)**
- 1 **tablespoon chopped parsley**
     Hot cooked rice
     Long, thin shreds of lemon peel (optional)

In a 1-cup glass measure, stir together broth, lemon juice, and cornstarch; set aside.

In a medium-size bowl, beat egg lightly. Add mint, garlic, flour, salt, pepper, and lamb; blend well. With dampened hands, shape lamb mixture into 12 meatballs, each about 1½ inches in diameter. Arrange meatballs in a circle on a microwave-safe plate. Cover and microwave on **HIGH (100%)** for 5 minutes. Drain off and discard juices. Give each meatball a quarter-turn, cover, and microwave on **HIGH (100%)** for 1 more minute or until meatballs are no longer pink in center; cut one to test. Let stand, covered, for 3 minutes.

Meanwhile, stir broth mixture; then microwave, uncovered, on **HIGH (100%)** for 2 minutes or until bubbly and slightly thickened, stirring after 1 minute. Stir in onion and parsley, cover, and let stand for 1 minute.

Spoon rice onto a platter. Arrange meatballs on top, then spoon sauce over all. Garnish with lemon peel, if desired. Makes 2 servings.

Per serving: 434 calories, 36 g protein, 7 g carbohydrates, 28 g total fat, 230 mg cholesterol, 659 mg sodium

With the right recipe and a little imagination, dinner abroad is as close as your own kitchen. Take a trip to Greece with our Minted Lamb Meatballs with Lemon Sauce (recipe on facing page)—tender, lightly sauced, and full of favorite Greek flavors.

LAMB CURRY

✳ ✳ ✳ ✳ ✳ ✳ ✳

Preparation time: About 15 minutes
Microwaving time: 35 to 37 minutes
Standing time: 5 minutes

Diced apple adds a fruity, mellow-sweet accent to this meaty curry. Serve curry over hot cooked rice or steaming, crunchy strands of spaghetti squash.

- 1¼ pounds lean boneless lamb
- 1 tablespoon *each* salad oil and curry powder
- ¼ teaspoon *each* ground ginger and sugar
- 1 medium-size onion, finely chopped
- 1 clove garlic, minced or pressed
- 1 medium-size Red Delicious apple, cored and diced
- 1 can (14½ oz.) tomatoes
  Hot cooked rice or spaghetti squash (to microwave spaghetti squash, follow directions on page 43)
  Plain yogurt
  Fresh cilantro (coriander) leaves

Trim and discard fat from lamb; then cut lamb into ¾-inch cubes and set aside.

In a 2½- to 3-quart microwave-safe casserole, stir together oil, curry powder, ginger, sugar, onion, and garlic. Cover and microwave on **HIGH (100%)** for 3 minutes, stirring after 2 minutes. Add lamb, cover, and microwave on **HIGH (100%)** for 4 minutes, stirring after 2 minutes. Stir in apple; then stir in tomatoes (break up with a spoon) and their liquid. Cover and microwave on **HIGH (100%)** for 8 minutes, stirring every 4 minutes. Then reduce power to **MEDIUM (50%)** and microwave, covered, for 20 to 22 minutes or until lamb is tender to bite; stir every 5 minutes. Let stand, covered, for 5 minutes.

To serve, spoon rice onto individual plates; then spoon curry over rice. Pass yogurt and cilantro at the table to add to individual servings. Makes 4 servings.

Per serving: 235 calories, 24 g protein, 12 g carbohydrates, 10 g total fat, 74 mg cholesterol, 243 mg sodium

CASUAL CASSOULET

✳ ✳ ✳ ✳ ✳ ✳ ✳

Preparation time: 10 to 15 minutes
Microwaving time: 11 to 15 minutes
Standing time: 3 minutes

Just a few minutes of microwaving are enough to meld garlic franks, lean boneless lamb, pinto beans, and vegetables into a flavorful cassoulet. To round out the meal, add crusty bread or rolls and a simple green salad.

- 1 small onion, thinly sliced
- 1 medium-size carrot, thinly sliced
- ½ teaspoon dry thyme leaves
- ¼ teaspoon dry rosemary
- 1 large shoulder lamb chop (about ½ lb.)
- ½ pound garlic frankfurters
- 1 can (about 15 oz.) pinto beans, drained
- 1 can (8 oz.) tomato sauce
  Chopped parsley

In a 2-quart microwave-safe casserole, combine onion and carrot; sprinkle with thyme and rosemary. Cover; microwave on **HIGH (100%)** for 3 to 4 minutes or until vegetables are tender when pierced, stirring after 2 minutes.

Cut lamb from bone; discard bone and fat, then cut meat into ¾-inch cubes. Cut frankfurters into ½-inch-thick slices. Stir meats into vegetables. Cover and microwave on **HIGH (100%)** for 3 to 4 minutes or until lamb is no longer pink on surface, stirring after 2 minutes. Mix in beans and tomato sauce. Cover and microwave on **HIGH (100%)** for 5 to 7 minutes or until beans are hot, stirring every 2 minutes. Sprinkle with parsley, cover, and let stand for 3 minutes. Makes 3 servings.

Per serving: 458 calories, 25 g protein, 32 g carbohydrates, 26 g total fat, 68 mg cholesterol, 1,936 mg sodium

SWISS JULIENNE OF VEAL

Preparation time: 15 to 20 minutes
Microwaving time: 15 to 17 minutes

A creamy mushroom-wine sauce coats tender strips of veal in this party entrée.

  1 **pound boneless veal cutlets, cut ½ inch thick**
     Paprika
  3 **tablespoons butter or margarine**
  ⅓ **cup sliced green onions (including tops)**
  ¼ **pound mushrooms, sliced**
  2 **tablespoons all-purpose flour**
  ¼ **cup dry white wine**
  ½ **cup whipping cream**
  ⅛ **teaspoon ground nutmeg**
     Salt and pepper
  1 **tablespoon finely chopped parsley**
  2 **tablespoons brandy**
     Hot cooked noodles (optional)

Carefully trim membrane away from veal. Place veal, one piece at a time, between 2 pieces of wax paper and pound with a flat-surfaced mallet until meat is evenly flattened to about ¼ inch thick. Sprinkle veal on each side with paprika. Cut into strips ¼ inch wide and 1½ inches long; set aside.

Place 2 tablespoons of the butter in a 7- by 11-inch microwave-safe baking dish; microwave, uncovered, on **HIGH (100%)** for about 35 seconds or until melted. Stir in onions and mushrooms; microwave, uncovered, on **HIGH (100%)** for 3 minutes, stirring after 1½ minutes. Stir in veal strips. Microwave, uncovered, on **HIGH (100%)** for 5 to 7 minutes, stirring after 3 minutes. Veal should no longer be pink in center; cut to test.

With a slotted spoon, lift veal and vegetables from drippings and place on a plate; cover and set aside. Pour drippings into a glass measure; you should have ½ cup (add water, if necessary).

Place remaining 1 tablespoon butter in baking dish; microwave, uncovered, on **HIGH (100%)** for about 30 seconds or until melted. Stir in flour and microwave, uncovered, on **HIGH (100%)** for 1 minute. Gradually stir in veal drippings, wine, and cream. Microwave, uncovered, on **HIGH (100%)** for 3 minutes or until smooth and thickened, stirring every minute.

Stir veal and vegetables into sauce; add nutmeg, season to taste with salt and pepper, and stir in parsley. Microwave, uncovered, on **HIGH (100%)** for 2 minutes or until hot throughout. Pour brandy into a small microwave-safe container; microwave, uncovered, on **HIGH (100%)** for 10 seconds or until warm to the touch. Ignite, pour over veal mixture, and stir until flames die down. Serve with noodles, if desired. Makes 4 servings.

Per serving: 309 calories, 26 g protein, 6 g carbohydrates, 20 g total fat, 145 mg cholesterol, 173 mg sodium

LIVER ITALIANO

Preparation time: About 5 minutes
Microwaving time: About 8 minutes
Standing time: 2 minutes

Use a special made-for-the-microwave browning dish to brown thin strips of liver; then add an herb-laced tomato sauce and top with cheese.

  ½ **teaspoon *each* dry basil and dry oregano leaves**
  1 **small can (about 8 oz.) spaghetti sauce**
  1 **pound beef liver, cut into ¼-inch-thick slices**
     Pepper
  1 **tablespoon olive oil**
  ¾ **cup shredded mozzarella cheese**
  ¼ **cup grated Parmesan cheese**

Stir basil and oregano into spaghetti sauce; set aside. Remove membrane from liver; cut liver into ¾- by 3-inch strips and sprinkle lightly with pepper.

Preheat a 2- to 2½-quart or 10-inch square microwave browning dish on **HIGH (100%)** for 4½ minutes. Using oven mitts, carefully remove dish to a heatproof surface. Pour oil into dish and tilt dish to coat bottom. Add liver and stir until sizzling stops. Then microwave, uncovered, on **HIGH (100%)** for 1 minute or until liver is browned on outside but still very pink inside, stirring after 30 seconds. Add spaghetti sauce mixture and stir well. Evenly sprinkle with mozzarella cheese, then with Parmesan cheese. Microwave, uncovered, on **HIGH (100%)** for 2 to 2½ minutes or until cheese is melted and mixture is heated through. Cover; let stand for 2 minutes. Makes 4 servings.

Per serving: 338 calories, 30 g protein, 17 g carbohydrates, 17 g total fat, 422 mg cholesterol, 537 mg sodium

A flowering sprig of rosemary makes a vivid garnish for thick halibut steaks topped with a smooth, spicy red pepper sauce. Serve Basque-inspired Halibut Pil-pil (recipe on page 52) with a salad and your favorite crusty dinner rolls—and be prepared for recipe requests!

Fish & Shellfish

Fish and shellfish are star microwave performers: they come from the oven moist and tender, with their delicate natural flavor intensified. Most seafood is agreeable to several microwaving methods. It can be cooked very simply, with no additional liquid or fat; butter-steamed with or without seasonings; or poached in a liquid. In any case, cooking time is brief. To avoid overcooking seafood, remove it from the oven when barely done, let it stand, and then test. If necessary, continue to microwave in 30-second increments.

Pictured on page 50

HALIBUT PIL-PIL

✳   ✳   ✳   ✳   ✳   ✳   ✳

Preparation time: About 15 minutes
Microwaving time: 10 to 11 minutes
Standing time: 3 minutes

To make this microwave adaptation of a Basque classic, you start by poaching halibut steaks in lemon juice and olive oil. Once the fish is done, purée the oil with garlic-seasoned red bell peppers to make a thin, mayonnaiselike sauce.

- ⅔ **cup olive oil**
- 3 **cloves garlic, halved**
- 2 **small red bell peppers, seeded and cut into thin strips**
- 2 **large or 4 small halibut or lingcod steaks (1½ to 2 lbs.** *total),* ***each about 1 inch thick***
- 2 **tablespoons dry white wine**
- ¼ **cup lemon juice**
- ½ **teaspoon crushed dried hot red chiles**
  Salt

Pour oil into a 9- by 13-inch microwave-safe baking dish. Add garlic and bell peppers. Microwave, uncovered, on **HIGH (100%)** for 6 minutes or until vegetables are soft, stirring after 3 minutes. Discard garlic; lift out pepper strips, place on paper towels, and let drain.

Rinse fish, pat dry, and place in hot oil, positioning thickest parts toward outside of dish. Cover and microwave on **HIGH (100%)** for 2 minutes. Stir together wine, lemon juice, and chiles; blend into oil in dish. Turn fish over and give each piece a half-turn. Cover and microwave on **HIGH (100%)** for 2 to 3 minutes. Let stand, covered, for 3 minutes. Fish should be just slightly translucent or wet inside; cut in thickest part to test.

With a wide spatula, carefully transfer fish to a hot serving dish; keep warm. Pour oil mixture from baking dish into a blender or food processor; add pepper strips and any fish juices that have collected in serving dish. Whirl until puréed and slightly thickened. Season sauce to taste with salt, then spoon over fish. Makes 4 servings.

Per serving: 512 calories, 34 g protein, 3 g carbohydrates, 40 g total fat, 52 mg cholesterol, 92 mg sodium

BURMESE FISH WITH SWEET ONIONS

✳   ✳   ✳   ✳   ✳   ✳   ✳

Preparation time: About 10 minutes
Microwaving time: 13 to 15 minutes
Standing time: 3 minutes

Serve this spicy Southeast Asian fish with hot cooked rice, steamed broccoli, and marinated cucumbers.

- 2 **tablespoons salad oil**
- 1 **large onion, thinly sliced**
- 1 **tablespoon minced fresh ginger**
- ¼ **teaspoon ground turmeric**
  About 4 teaspoons seeded, minced fresh hot chile, such as jalapeño
- 1½ **tablespoons soy sauce**
- 1 **teaspoon sugar**
- ⅛ **teaspoon pepper**
- 2 **large or 4 small halibut or swordfish steaks (1½ to 2 lbs.** *total),* ***each about 1 inch thick***

In a 7- by 11-inch microwave-safe baking dish, stir together oil, onion, ginger, turmeric, and 3 teaspoons of the chile (or more, for a hotter flavor). Microwave, uncovered, on **HIGH (100%)** for 8 to 10 minutes or until onion is very soft, stirring every 4 minutes. Stir in soy, sugar, and pepper.

Rinse fish and pat dry. Push onion mixture aside; lay fish in dish, positioning thickest parts toward outside of dish. Then spoon onion mixture in a band over fish. Cover and microwave on **HIGH (100%)** for 3 minutes; give each piece of fish a half-turn. Cover and microwave on **HIGH (100%)** for 2 minutes. Let stand, covered, for 3 minutes. Fish should be just slightly translucent or wet inside; cut in thickest part to test. Sprinkle any remaining chile over fish, if desired. Makes 4 servings.

Per serving: 261 calories, 34 g protein, 5 g carbohydrates, 11 g total fat, 52 mg cholesterol, 474 mg sodium

✳ SEAFOOD COOKING CHART ✳

CAUTION: To prevent overcooking, use shortest cooking time; then let seafood stand before testing for doneness. If necessary, continue to microwave in 30-second increments. To cover seafood for cooking, you may use heavy-duty plastic wrap, the container lid, or (to cover loosely) wax paper.

SEAFOOD	PREPARATION	COOKING TIME (CT) STANDING TIME (ST)
Fish steaks or fillets Red snapper or other rockfish, Greenland turbot, sole, halibut, sea bass, salmon; ½ to ¾ inch thick (1 lb.)	If frozen, thaw completely. Rinse and pat dry. In a greased 7- by 11-inch microwave-safe baking dish, arrange fish in an even layer with thickest portions toward outside of dish. If desired, brush with melted butter or margarine and season with paprika, dry dill weed, or lemon juice. Cover.	**CT:** 3–4 minutes per lb. Microwave on **HIGH (100%)**, giving fish pieces or dish ½ turn after 2 minutes. **ST:** 3 minutes, covered. Fish should be just slightly translucent or wet inside; cut to test.
Trout, whole (cleaned and dressed) 1 or 2 (8–10 oz. *each*)	If frozen, thaw completely. Rinse and pat dry. Stuff with lemon or onion slices, if desired. In a greased 7- by 11-inch microwave-safe baking dish, arrange fish lengthwise, with backbones toward outside of dish. Brush with melted butter or margarine. Cover.	**CT:** 1 trout 2½–3½ minutes 2 trout 5–7 minutes Microwave on **HIGH (100%)**, turning fish over and bringing cooked portions to inside of dish halfway through cooking. **ST:** 3 minutes, covered. Fish should be just slightly translucent or wet inside; cut to test.
Hard-shell clams in shell, suitable for steaming 12 clams	Scrub well. On a 10-inch microwave-safe pie plate or serving plate, arrange clams in a circle, with hinge sides toward edge of plate. Cover loosely.	**CT:** 3–4 minutes Microwave on **HIGH (100%)** until shells pop open. Lift out opened clams; continue to microwave remaining clams, checking at 30-second intervals. **ST:** 1 minute, covered.
Crab in shell (cleaned, cooked, and cracked) 1 large (about 2 lbs.)	In a 7- by 11-inch microwave-safe baking dish, arrange crab pieces with meaty portions toward outside of dish. Brush with melted butter or margarine. Cover.	**CT:** 2–3 minutes Microwave on **HIGH (100%)**. Meat in shells should be heated through. **ST:** 1–2 minutes, covered.
Oysters in shell Eastern, 10–12 Pacific, 8 medium-size	Same as for hard-shell clams in shell.	**CT:** 4–5 minutes Microwave on **HIGH (100%)** until shells pop open. Edges of oysters should be curled. **ST:** 2 minutes, covered.
Oysters, shucked Eastern, 8–10 Pacific, small, 1 jar (10 oz.)	On a 10-inch microwave-safe pie plate or serving plate, arrange oysters in a circle. Drizzle with juices and melted butter or margarine. Cover.	**CT:** 3 minutes Microwave on **HIGH (100%)**, turning over after 1½ minutes. Oysters should be heated through and edges curled. **ST:** 1–2 minutes, covered.
Scallops (1 lb.)	Rinse well; if large, cut in half. Place in a 1½-quart microwave-safe casserole. Drizzle with melted butter or margarine and dry white wine or lemon juice. Cover.	**CT:** About 3 minutes Microwave on **HIGH (100%)**, stirring after 1½ minutes. **ST:** 4 minutes, covered. Scallops should be opaque throughout; cut to test.
Shrimp, raw, medium-large 31–35 (1 lb.)	Rinse well. Shell and devein, if desired. On a flat 12-inch microwave-safe plate, arrange shrimp in a single layer with thickest parts toward edge of plate. Cover.	**CT:** About 4 minutes Microwave on **HIGH (100%)**, bringing cooked portion to inside of plate after 2 minutes. **ST:** 2 minutes, covered. Shrimp should be opaque throughout; cut to test.

Pictured on facing page

SEA BASS WITH GINGER

✳   ✳   ✳   ✳   ✳   ✳   ✳

Preparation time: About 15 minutes
Microwaving time: 2 to 4 minutes
Standing time: 3 minutes

Pepped up with orange and fresh ginger, sea bass makes a light, lean, and flavorful entrée. Serve a colorful vegetable alongside—perhaps Chinese pea pods or buttered baby carrots.

    ¾   to 1 pound white sea bass fillets
        (*each* 1 to 1½ inches thick)
    2   tablespoons orange juice
    4   teaspoons soy sauce
    2   teaspoons finely shredded fresh ginger
    1   teaspoon finely shredded orange peel
        Fresh cilantro (coriander) sprigs
        Orange wedges

To butterfly fish, cut each fillet in half horizontally almost all the way through; open fillets out flat. On both sides of each opened-out fillet, make cross-wise cuts at 1-inch intervals; cut toward center of fillet, leaving about a 1½-inch-wide strip uncut at center. Rinse fish and pat dry.

Set fish pieces in a 9- by 13-inch microwave-safe baking dish and drizzle evenly with orange juice and soy. Sprinkle ginger and orange peel evenly over fish. Cover and microwave on **HIGH (100%)** for 2 minutes. Let stand, covered, for 3 minutes. Fish should be just slightly translucent or wet inside; cut in thickest part to test. If necessary, cover and microwave on **HIGH (100%)** for 1 to 2 more minutes, testing for doneness every 30 seconds.

Arrange fish on individual plates and garnish with cilantro and orange wedges. Makes 2 servings.

Per serving: 210 calories, 38 g protein, 3 g carbohydrates, 4 g total fat, 82 mg cholesterol, 823 mg sodium

POACHED MONKFISH EN CASSEROLE

✳   ✳   ✳   ✳   ✳   ✳   ✳

Preparation time: About 15 minutes
Microwaving time: 14 to 19 minutes
Standing time: 2 minutes

Thanks to its sweet, lobsterlike flavor, monkfish is sometimes called "poor man's lobster." Here, the lean, firm-textured fillets are presented in a creamy sauce and topped with Swiss cheese.

    1½ pounds monkfish fillets
        About ½ cup dry white wine or regular-
        strength chicken broth
    ½   pound mushrooms, sliced
    6   tablespoons butter or margarine
    ⅛   teaspoon ground nutmeg
    2   tablespoons all-purpose flour
        Salt
    1½ cups (6 oz.) shredded Swiss cheese
        Chopped parsley

If necessary, remove silvery membrane from fish: slide a knife underneath membrane to loosen it, then pull membrane off from one side. Rinse fish and pat dry. Fold narrow end of fillets under to make evenly thick pieces.

Place fish and ½ cup of the wine in a 2- to 2½-quart microwave-safe casserole. Cover and micro-wave on **HIGH (100%)** for 6 to 8 minutes, giving dish a half-turn after 4 minutes. Fish should be just slightly translucent or wet inside; cut in thickest part to test. Pour off and reserve liquid.

In a 4-cup glass measure, combine mushrooms, 2 tablespoons of the butter, and nutmeg. Cover and microwave on **HIGH (100%)** for 3 to 5 minutes or until mushrooms are limp, stirring every 2 minutes. With a slotted spoon, lift out mushrooms and ar-range over fish in casserole.

Add reserved cooking liquid to mushroom liq-uid; add wine, if needed, to make 1 cup. Set aside.

Place remaining ¼ cup butter in another 4-cup glass measure; microwave, uncovered, on **HIGH (100%)** for about 45 seconds or until melted. Using a wire whisk, blend in flour, then liquid. Micro-wave, uncovered, on **HIGH (100%)** for 1½ to 2 min-utes or until thick, stirring every 30 seconds. Season to taste with salt.

Pour sauce over fish and mushrooms; top with cheese. Microwave, uncovered, on **HIGH (100%)** for 2½ to 3 minutes or until fish is heated through, giving dish a half-turn after 1½ minutes. Let stand, uncovered, for 2 minutes. Garnish with parsley. Makes 4 servings.

Per serving: 472 calories, 39 g protein, 7 g carbohydrates, 32 g total fat, 128 mg cholesterol, 321 mg sodium

Dinner's as pretty as a picture when you serve snowy white
Sea Bass with Ginger (recipe on facing page). The thick fillets are butterflied
and slashed crosswise, then lightly seasoned with orange,
soy, and ginger before microwaving.

ROCKFISH FLORENTINE

Preparation time: 15 minutes
Microwaving time: 9 to 11 minutes
Standing time: 3 minutes

Cloaked with a tart and creamy sauce, these thick rockfish fillets are served on a bed of cooked fresh spinach.

- ⅔ **cup sour cream with chives (or plain sour cream)**
- 3 **tablespoons mayonnaise**
- 2 **tablespoons** *each* **all-purpose flour and lemon juice**
- ¼ **teaspoon dry dill weed**
- 1½ **to 2 pounds spinach, rinsed well**
- 1 **pound rockfish fillets** (*each* **about ½ inch thick)**
  Salt and pepper
  Paprika
  Snipped chives

In a small bowl, beat together sour cream, mayonnaise, flour, lemon juice, and dill weed with a wire whisk until smoothly blended. Set aside.

Remove and discard stems and any yellow or wilted leaves from spinach. Place spinach in a 3-quart microwave-safe casserole. Cover and microwave on **HIGH (100%)** for 4 to 5 minutes or until wilted but still bright green, stirring after 2½ minutes. Cover and set aside.

Rinse fish, pat dry, and cut into serving-size pieces. Place in a 7- by 11-inch microwave-safe baking dish, positioning thickest parts toward outside of dish; season to taste with salt and pepper. Microwave, uncovered, on **HIGH (100%)** for 3 minutes. Give dish a half-turn and spread each fillet with sour cream mixture. Microwave, uncovered, on **HIGH (100%)** for 2 to 3 minutes; then cover and let stand for 3 minutes. Fish should be just slightly translucent or wet inside; cut in thickest part to test.

While fish is standing, drain spinach and arrange on a warm platter. Top with fish; spoon any sauce remaining in baking dish over fish. Sprinkle with paprika and chives. Makes 4 servings.

Per serving: 323 calories, 29 g protein, 12 g carbohydrates, 19 g total fat, 63 mg cholesterol, 306 mg sodium

ROCKFISH AMANDINE

Preparation time: About 10 minutes
Microwaving time: 11 to 14 minutes
Standing time: 3 minutes

For a simple but elegant entrée, microwave moist rockfish fillets in a pungent garlic-lemon butter, then top with toasted almonds just before serving.

- 2 **tablespoons slivered blanched almonds**
- ¼ **cup butter or margarine**
- 3 **cloves garlic, minced or pressed**
- 1 **tablespoon** *each* **lemon juice and chopped parsley**
- ¼ **teaspoon** *each* **paprika and grated lemon peel**
- ¾ **to 1 pound rockfish or lingcod fillets** (*each* **about ½ inch thick)**
  Lemon wedges

Spread almonds in a 9-inch microwave-safe baking dish. Microwave, uncovered, on **HIGH (100%)** for 6 to 8 minutes or until almonds are golden, stirring every 2 minutes. Set aside.

Place butter, garlic, lemon juice, parsley, paprika, and lemon peel in a 1-cup glass measure. Microwave, uncovered, on **HIGH (100%)** for 2 minutes or until heated through. Set aside.

Rinse fish, pat dry, and cut into serving-size pieces. Place in a 7- by 11-inch microwave-safe baking dish, positioning thickest parts toward outside of dish. Pour butter mixture over fish and turn to coat all sides. Microwave, uncovered, on **HIGH (100%)** for 3 to 4 minutes, giving dish a half-turn after 1½ minutes. Cover and let stand for 3 minutes. Fish should be just slightly translucent or wet inside; cut in thickest part to test. Arrange fish on a warm platter. Pour juices remaining in baking dish over fish; sprinkle with almonds and garnish with lemon wedges. Makes 3 servings.

Per serving: 300 calories, 26 g protein, 3 g carbohydrates, 20 g total fat, 88 mg cholesterol, 239 mg sodium

SOLE FILLETS WITH CAPERS

✳   ✳   ✳   ✳   ✳   ✳   ✳

Preparation time: 5 to 10 minutes
Microwaving time: About 2 minutes
Standing time: 1 to 2 minutes

Microwaving a single serving of thin sole fillets takes only a minute or two. If you're serving several people, microwave each serving separately; while one plate of fish is standing, you can slip the next one into the oven.

- ½ **pound sole fillets**
- 1 **teaspoon lemon juice**
- 1 **tablespoon finely snipped chives**
- ½ **teaspoon** *each* **finely shredded lemon peel and drained capers**
- ⅛ **teaspoon crushed dried hot red chiles**
  Lemon wedges
  Salt and pepper

Rinse fish and pat dry. Place fish in a single layer on a 9- to 10-inch microwave-safe plate, overlapping thin edges of fillets. Drizzle with lemon juice and sprinkle with chives, lemon peel, capers, and chiles. Cover and microwave on **HIGH (100%)** for 1½ to 2 minutes; then let stand, covered, for 1 to 2 minutes. Fish should be just slightly translucent or wet inside; cut in thickest part to test. Garnish with lemon wedges; season to taste with salt and pepper. Makes 1 serving.

Per serving: 210 calories, 43 g protein, .7 g carbohydrates, 3 g total fat, 109 mg cholesterol, 222 mg sodium

SHARK STEAKS WITH MUSHROOMS

✳   ✳   ✳   ✳   ✳   ✳   ✳

Preparation time: 10 to 20 minutes
Marinating time: 30 minutes to 1 hour
Microwaving time: 8 minutes
Standing time: 3 minutes

Boneless, mild-flavored shark steaks have a firm, moist, meaty texture. Here, they're enhanced by a lemon marinade, then served with a mushroom topping and a sprinkling of chives.

- 2 **tablespoons** *each* **lemon juice and dry white wine**
- 1 **clove garlic, minced or pressed**
- ¼ **teaspoon dry oregano leaves**
- ¼ **teaspoon fennel seeds, crushed**
- ⅛ **teaspoon pepper**
- 1 **tablespoon olive oil or salad oil**
- 2 **shark steaks (¾ to 1 lb.** *total***), *each* about 1 inch thick**
- ¼ **pound mushrooms, thinly sliced**
  Salt
  Snipped chives

In a 9-inch square microwave-safe baking dish, stir together lemon juice, wine, garlic, oregano, fennel seeds, pepper, and oil. Rinse fish and pat dry, then add to marinade and turn several times to coat well. Let marinate at room temperature for 30 min-

utes to 1 hour, turning fish over every 15 minutes. Drain marinade into a microwave-safe bowl and stir in mushrooms; set aside.

Arrange fish with thickest parts toward outside of dish. Cover and microwave on **HIGH (100%)** for 5 minutes, giving each steak a half-turn after 3 minutes. Let stand, covered, for 3 minutes. Fish should be just slightly translucent or wet inside; cut in thickest part to test.

While fish is standing, microwave mushroom mixture, uncovered, on **HIGH (100%)** for 3 minutes, stirring after 1½ minutes. Season to taste with salt. Transfer fish to a serving plate; top with mushroom mixture and sprinkle with chives. Makes 2 servings.

Per serving: 341 calories, 43 g protein, 5 g carbohydrates, 16 g total fat, 102 mg cholesterol, 165 mg sodium

No need to serve a salad with this entrée—the greens are part of the main course. Salmon Steaks on Wilted Chicory Salad (recipe on facing page) features hot, herb-seasoned salmon on a bed of crisp, curly chicory and mushrooms in a light vinaigrette.

Pictured on facing page

SALMON STEAKS ON WILTED CHICORY SALAD

✳   ✳   ✳   ✳   ✳   ✳   ✳

Preparation time: 20 to 25 minutes
Microwaving time: 8 to 9 minutes
Standing time: 3 minutes

Nippy-tasting, curly-leafed chicory provides a dramatic contrast in color and flavor to these moist, thyme-accented salmon steaks.

- 6 ounces mushrooms, thinly sliced
- 4½ tablespoons extra-virgin olive oil
- 3 tablespoons thinly sliced green onions (including tops)
- 1½ tablespoons red wine vinegar
- 2 cloves garlic, minced or pressed
- 3 tablespoons minced fresh thyme leaves or 1½ tablespoons dry thyme leaves
- 4 salmon steaks (8 oz. each), each 1 inch thick
- 6 cups bite-size pieces chicory (curly endive), washed and crisped
  Salt and pepper

Place mushrooms and 1½ tablespoons of the oil in a 3-quart microwave-safe casserole. Cover; microwave on **HIGH (100%)** for 4 minutes, stirring after 2 minutes. In a bowl, mix remaining 3 tablespoons oil, onions, vinegar, garlic, and thyme.

Rinse fish; pat dry. Coat each piece with some of the oil mixture; arrange in a 7- by 11-inch microwave-safe baking dish, positioning thickest parts toward outside of dish. Cover and microwave on **HIGH (100%)** for 4 to 5 minutes, giving each fish steak a half-turn after 2 minutes. Let stand, covered, for 3 minutes. Fish should be just slightly translucent or wet inside; cut in thickest part to test.

Add any remaining oil mixture to mushrooms; stir in chicory, mixing lightly to coat greens evenly. Spoon chicory mixture onto 4 individual plates; top each serving with a salmon steak. Season to taste with salt and pepper. Makes 4 servings.

Per serving: 464 calories, 40 g protein, 17 g carbohydrates, 28 g total fat, 96 mg cholesterol, 201 mg sodium

WALLA WALLA SALMON

✳   ✳   ✳   ✳   ✳   ✳   ✳

Preparation time: About 10 minutes
Microwaving time: 24 to 30 minutes
Standing time: 3 minutes

Sliced almonds, coconut, and sweet onions accented with teriyaki sauce make unusual—but delectable —toppings for meaty salmon fillets.

- ¼ cup sliced almonds
- ¼ cup sweetened shredded coconut
  Teriyaki Sauce (recipe follows)
- 1 large mild onion, thinly sliced
- 1½ tablespoons salad oil
- 4 pieces salmon fillet (about 6 oz. each)
  Lemon wedges

Spread almonds in a 7- by 11-inch microwave-safe baking dish. Microwave, uncovered, on **HIGH (100%)** for 6 to 8 minutes or until almonds are golden, stirring every 2 minutes. Add coconut and microwave, uncovered, on **HIGH (100%)** for 2 to 3 more minutes or until coconut is toasted, stirring after 1½ minutes. Spoon almonds and coconut onto a plate and set aside.

Prepare Teriyaki Sauce. Pour 3 tablespoons of the sauce into baking dish; stir in onion and 1 tablespoon of the oil. Cover and microwave on **HIGH (100%)** for 8 to 10 minutes or until onion is very soft, stirring every 4 minutes. Cover; set aside.

Rinse fish and pat dry. Preheat a 2- to 2½-quart or 10-inch square microwave browning dish on **HIGH (100%)** for 4½ minutes. Using oven mitts, carefully remove dish to a heatproof surface. Add remaining 1½ teaspoons oil; tilt dish to coat bottom. Arrange fish in dish, skin side up. When sizzling stops, turn fish over. Microwave, uncovered, on **HIGH (100%)** for 3 to 4 minutes, brushing with remaining Teriyaki Sauce after 1½ minutes. Cover; let stand for 3 minutes. Fish should be just slightly translucent or wet inside; cut in thickest part to test.

Top fish with onion mixture, almonds, and coconut. Serve with lemon wedges. Makes 4 servings.

Teriyaki Sauce. Mix 3 tablespoons **soy sauce,** 2 tablespoons **dry sherry** or water, and 1 tablespoon *each* **Oriental sesame oil** and minced **fresh ginger.**

Per serving: 399 calories, 36 g protein, 9 g carbohydrates, 24 g total fat, 94 mg cholesterol, 861 mg sodium

ZESTY
SAUCES &
CONDIMENTS

When you want to dress up any simply cooked meat or poultry—whether from grill, oven, skillet, or microwave—just serve it with one of these bold embellishments.

Always prepare our sauces and condiments in a deep container to protect the oven walls from splashes and spatters. And remember that the container will become quite hot—so use potholders to remove it from the microwave, then place it on a heatproof surface to cool.

HEAVY-DUTY BARBECUE SAUCE

Preparation time: About 10 minutes
Microwaving time: 7 minutes
Standing time: 5 minutes

Use this hearty, richly flavored sauce as a baste for steaks, spareribs, or chicken parts during the last 10 to 15 minutes of cooking. Or serve it hot, as a sauce for simmered beef brisket.

- 1 **tablespoon salad oil**
- 1 **clove garlic, minced or pressed**
- 1 **can (6 oz.) tomato paste**
- ½ **cup light molasses**
- ¼ **cup** *each* **prepared mustard and soy sauce**
- 3 **tablespoons Worcestershire**
- 2 **tablespoons red wine vinegar**
- 2 **teaspoons ground sage**
- ½ **to 1 teaspoon liquid hot pepper seasoning**
- ½ **to 1 teaspoon pepper**

Pour oil into a deep 3-quart microwave-safe bowl. Add garlic; microwave, uncovered, on **HIGH (100%)** for 2 minutes, stirring after 1 minute. Stir in tomato paste, molasses, mustard, soy, Worcestershire, vinegar, sage, hot pepper seasoning, and pepper. Microwave, uncovered, on **HIGH**

(100%) for 5 minutes, stirring after 3 minutes. Cover and let stand for 5 minutes to blend flavors. If made ahead, let cool; then cover and refrigerate for up to 2 weeks. Bring to room temperature or reheat before using. Makes 1¾ to 2 cups.

Per tablespoon: 27 calories, .5 g protein, 5 g carbohydrates, .6 g total fat, 0 mg cholesterol, 229 mg sodium

CHINESE PLUM SAUCE

Preparation time: About 10 minutes
Microwaving time: 20 minutes

This distinctive spicy-sweet sauce enhances duck, chicken, and any cut of pork—roast, chops, or ribs. Brush it over the meat or poultry during the last 10 minutes of cooking.

- 1 **can (about 1 lb.) whole purple plums**
- ¼ **cup water**
- 1 **tablespoon salad oil**
- 1 **small onion, finely chopped**
- ½ **teaspoon Chinese five-spice or** ⅛ **teaspoon** *each* **ground anise, ginger, cloves, and cinnamon**
- ¼ **teaspoon** *each* **dry mustard, ground cumin, and ground cinnamon**
- ⅛ **teaspoon pepper**
- ¼ **cup tomato-based chili sauce**
- 1½ **teaspoons** *each* **soy sauce and Worcestershire**
- ¼ **teaspoon liquid hot pepper seasoning**
- 1½ **teaspoons rice wine vinegar**

Drain plums, reserving ⅔ cup of the syrup (discard remaining syrup). Remove pits from plums. In a blender or food processor, combine pitted plums, reserved ⅔ cup syrup, and water; whirl until puréed. Set aside.

Pour oil into a deep 3-quart microwave-safe bowl; add onion and microwave, uncovered, on **HIGH (100%)** for 5 minutes, stirring after 2½ minutes. Stir in five-spice, mustard, cumin, cinnamon, pepper, chili sauce, soy, Worcestershire, hot pepper seasoning, and plum purée. Microwave, uncovered, on **HIGH (100%)** for 15 minutes or until reduced to about 1½ cups, stirring every 3 minutes. Stir in vinegar. If made ahead, let cool; then cover and refrigerate for up to 2 weeks. Reheat before using. Makes about 1½ cups.

Per tablespoon: 21 calories, .2 g protein, 4 g carbohydrates, .6 g total fat, 0 mg cholesterol, 68 mg sodium

CURRY SAUCE

Preparation time: 5 to 10 minutes
Microwaving time: 15 to 20 minutes

Yesterday's meat, poultry, or seafood turns into party food when stirred into our quick curry sauce. The recipe makes 2 cups—enough for 3 to 4 cups of cubed meat.

- 3 **tablespoons butter or margarine**
- 1 **large onion, finely chopped**
- 2 **cloves garlic, minced or pressed**
- 1 **tablespoon curry powder**
- ¼ **teaspoon ground ginger**
- 3 **tablespoons all-purpose flour**
- 1 **can (14½ oz.) regular-strength beef or chicken broth**

Place butter in a 3-quart microwave-safe casserole. Microwave, uncovered, on **HIGH (100%)** for about 40 seconds or until melted. Stir in onion and garlic; microwave, uncovered, on **HIGH (100%)** for 8 to 10 minutes or until onion is very soft, stirring every 4 minutes. Stir in curry powder, ginger, and flour; microwave, uncovered, on **HIGH (100%)** for 1 to 2 minutes or until bubbly. Gradually stir in broth. Microwave, uncovered, on **HIGH (100%)** for 5 to 7 minutes or until thickened, stirring every minute. Makes about 2 cups.

Per ½ cup: 129 calories, 2 g protein, 9 g carbohydrates, 9 g total fat, 23 mg cholesterol, 465 mg sodium

APPLE CHUTNEY

* * * * *

Preparation time: About 30 minutes
Microwaving time: 16 minutes

Offer big spoonfuls of this spicy condiment with roasted or barbecued meats, poultry, or fish; or serve it with curried lamb or chicken.

1   **pound Newtown Pippin apples, peeled, cored, and chopped**
½   **small onion, chopped**
½   **lemon (unpeeled), seeded and finely chopped**
½   **small red bell pepper, seeded and chopped**
2   **tablespoons minced fresh ginger**
1   **clove garlic, minced or pressed**
⅓   **cup apple cider vinegar**
⅔   **cup firmly packed brown sugar**
⅛   **teaspoon ground red pepper (cayenne)**
¼   **teaspoon salt**

In a large bowl, combine apples, onion, lemon, bell pepper, ginger, and garlic. Set aside.

In a deep 3-quart microwave-safe bowl, stir together vinegar, sugar, ground red pepper, and salt. Microwave, uncovered, on **HIGH**

(100%) for 1 minute or until sugar is dissolved, stirring after 30 seconds.

Stir in apple mixture. Microwave, uncovered, on **HIGH (100%)** for 15 minutes or until mixture is reduced to about 2 cups, stirring every 3 minutes. Let cool. If made ahead, cover and refrigerate for up to 3 weeks. Makes about 2 cups.

Per tablespoon: 26 calories, .03 g protein, 7 g carbohydrates, .03 g total fat, 0 mg cholesterol,

RED ONION MARMALADE

* * * * *

Preparation time: 5 to 10 minutes
Microwaving time: 23 to 25 minutes

Sweet-sour and spicy, this unusual condiment is an ideal accompaniment for pan-browned sausages.

1   **tablespoon butter or margarine**
1   **pound red onions, thinly sliced**
3   **tablespoons sugar**
¼   **teaspoon pepper**
½   **cup dry red wine**
2   **tablespoons red wine vinegar**

Place butter in a deep 3-quart microwave-safe bowl; microwave, uncovered, on **HIGH (100%)** for about 30 seconds or until melted. Stir in onions, sugar, and pepper. Cover and microwave on **HIGH (100%)** for 10 to 12 minutes or until onions are very soft, stirring every 5 minutes.

Add wine and vinegar. Microwave, uncovered, on **HIGH (100%)** for 12 minutes or until liquid has evaporated, stirring every 5 minutes. Serve warm. If made ahead, let cool; then cover and refrigerate for up to 3 days. Reheat before serving. Makes about 1¼ cups.

Per ¼ cup: 83 calories, 1 g protein, 15 g carbohydrates, 3 g total fat, 6 mg cholesterol, 27 mg sodium

SWEET-SOUR ORANGE PICKLES

* * * * *

Preparation time: About 10 minutes
Microwaving time: 28 to 35 minutes

Tangy, fragrant citrus pickles cook quickly and evenly when prepared in a microwave oven. Try them as an accompaniment to meat or poultry, or serve with hearty sandwiches.

2   **medium-size thin-skinned oranges such as Valencia, ends trimmed**
1½   **cups water**
2   **cinnamon sticks (*each* about 3 inches long)**
¼   **teaspoon *each* salt, ground allspice, and ground nutmeg**
½   **teaspoon ground ginger**
⅓   **cup *each* sugar and currants**
⅔   **cup apple cider vinegar**
¼   **to ½ teaspoon crushed dried hot red chiles**

Cut oranges in half lengthwise, then thinly slice crosswise. Discard any seeds. Place oranges and water in a 3-quart microwave-safe casserole. Cover and microwave on **HIGH (100%)** for 12 to 15 minutes or until orange peel is tender when pierced, stirring every 5 minutes. Drain off and discard liquid.

To oranges, add cinnamon sticks, salt, allspice, nutmeg, ginger, sugar, currants, vinegar, and chiles. Stir to blend. Cover and microwave on **HIGH (100%)** for 16 to 20 minutes or until orange peel is very tender when pierced and almost all liquid has evaporated, stirring every 4 minutes.

Serve warm or at room temperature. If made ahead, let cool; then cover and refrigerate for up to 3 weeks. Makes about 2 cups.

Per ¼ cup: 91 calories, 1 g protein, 27 g carbohydrates, .21 g total fat, 0 mg cholesterol, 92 mg sodium

Pictured on facing page

TROUT WITH VEGETABLES

✳   ✳   ✳   ✳   ✳   ✳   ✳

Preparation time: About 15 minutes
Microwaving time: 11 to 13 minutes
Standing time: 3 minutes

Steamed atop a bed of colorful vegetables, a trio of fresh trout can become a banquet for three in just minutes. Alongside, offer buttered potatoes and a chilled dry white wine.

  2 **tablespoons butter or margarine**
  1 **small onion, thinly sliced**
  1 **clove garlic, minced or pressed**
  1 **small red bell pepper, seeded and cut into ⅛-inch-wide strips**
  1 **pound zucchini or yellow crookneck squash (or ½ lb. of *each* kind), cut into ⅛-inch-thick slices**
  1 **tablespoon fresh tarragon leaves or ¼ teaspoon dry tarragon**
  ½ **teaspoon freshly ground pepper**
  3 **cleaned whole trout (8 to 10 oz. *each*)**
     Lemon wedges
     Fresh tarragon sprigs
     Salt

Place butter on a 10-inch rimmed microwave-safe plate; microwave, uncovered, on **HIGH (100%)** for about 35 seconds or until melted. Stir in onion, garlic, bell pepper, zucchini, tarragon leaves, and pepper.

Rinse fish and pat dry. Then arrange, heads pointing in same direction and cavity sides down, over vegetable mixture; lean fish against each other. Cover and microwave on **HIGH (100%)** for 4 minutes. Turn fish over so heads point in opposite direction; cover and microwave on **HIGH (100%)** for 6 to 8 minutes. Let stand, covered, for 3 minutes. Fish should be just slightly translucent or wet inside; cut in thickest part to test.

Garnish with lemon wedges and tarragon sprigs. Season to taste with salt. Makes 3 servings.

Per serving: 297 calories, 30 g protein, 7 g carbohydrates, 17 g total fat, 97 mg cholesterol, 153 mg sodium

STEAMED TROUT WITH LETTUCE & PEAS

✳   ✳   ✳   ✳   ✳   ✳   ✳

Preparation time: About 20 minutes
Microwaving time: 9 to 11 minutes
Standing time: 3 minutes

Succulent whole trout and mint-seasoned tiny peas take a steam bath right on the serving plate for this eye-catching entrée. You might accompany the tender fish and vegetables with crisp, sesame-crusted bread sticks.

  3 **tablespoons chopped fresh mint**
  1 **tablespoon finely shredded lemon peel**
  1 **clove garlic, minced or pressed**
  1 **cup frozen tiny peas, thawed**
  3 **cups shredded romaine lettuce leaves**
     Salt and pepper
  4 **cleaned whole trout or baby salmon (8 to 10 oz. *each*)**
  1 **tablespoon lemon juice**
     Lemon wedges

In a bowl, mix mint, lemon peel, garlic, peas, and lettuce; season to taste with salt and pepper. Pat mixture gently into a mound on a 10-inch rimmed microwave-safe plate.

Rinse fish and pat dry. Then arrange, heads pointing in same direction and cavity sides down, over pea mixture; lean fish against each other.

Cover and microwave on **HIGH (100%)** for 4 minutes. Turn fish over so heads point in opposite direction; cover and microwave on **HIGH (100%)** for 5 to 7 minutes. Let stand, covered, for 3 minutes. Fish should be just slightly translucent or wet inside; cut in thickest part to test. Sprinkle with lemon juice. Transfer trout to individual plates and spoon lettuce mixture alongside. Garnish with lemon wedges. Makes 4 servings.

Per serving: 239 calories, 31 g protein, 7 g carbohydrates, 9 g total fat, 78 mg cholesterol, 138 mg sodium

Silvery and succulent, these whole fresh trout rest atop a bright medley
of summer squash, red bell pepper, and onion. If you have a microwave-safe
plate pretty enough to go to the table, cook Trout with Vegetables (recipe
on facing page) right on it—you'll save on cleanup.

VEGETABLE-TOPPED FISH FILLETS

✳   ✳   ✳   ✳   ✳   ✳   ✳

Preparation time: About 15 minutes
Microwaving time: About 16 minutes
Standing time: 9 to 13 minutes

With the microwave's help, frozen fish fillets can go from freezer to dinner table in half an hour. Each fillet is crowned with a creamy vegetable topping.

>2 tablespoons butter or margarine
>½ cup finely grated carrot
>3 tablespoons thinly sliced green onions (including tops)
>2 tablespoons lemon juice
>1 small package (3 oz.) cream cheese, at room temperature
>1 tablespoon minced parsley
>¼ teaspoon ground white pepper
>1 package (12 oz.) frozen cod or sole fillets
>Thin tomato wedges

Place butter in a small microwave-safe bowl. Microwave, uncovered, on **HIGH (100%)** for about 35 seconds or until melted. Stir in carrot and onions; microwave, uncovered, on **HIGH (100%)** for 4 minutes or until soft, stirring after 2 minutes. Let cool; then add lemon juice, cream cheese, parsley, and white pepper. Blend well and set aside.

Stack 2 paper towels on oven floor. Place unopened package of fish on towels and microwave on **MEDIUM (50%)** for 5 minutes, turning package over after 2 minutes. Open package; let stand for 6 to 10 minutes or until fish is completely thawed. If fish is still frozen in center, cover package with paper towels; microwave on **MEDIUM (50%)** for 1 more minute, then let stand until thawed.

Separate fish into fillets, rinse, and pat dry. Place in a 9-inch square microwave-safe baking dish, positioning thickest parts toward outside of dish. Cover and microwave on **HIGH (100%)** for 3 minutes. Give dish a half-turn, then spread cheese mixture evenly over each fillet. Microwave, uncovered, on **MEDIUM-HIGH (70–80%)** for 2 minutes. Let stand, covered, for 3 minutes. Fish should be just slightly translucent or wet inside; cut in thickest part to test. Top each fillet with a few tomato wedges. Makes 2 servings.

Per serving: 420 calories, 36 g protein, 5 g carbohydrates, 28 g total fat, 159 mg cholesterol, 391 mg sodium

SEASIDE BURRITOS

✳   ✳   ✳   ✳   ✳   ✳   ✳

Preparation time: 15 to 20 minutes
Microwaving time: About 5 minutes
Standing time: 3 minutes

Inspired by the tacos served in Mexican seaside villages, these light burritos feature moist chunks of poached fish tucked into flour tortillas.

>Salsa Fresca (recipe follows)
>1½ tablespoons lemon juice
>¼ teaspoon crushed dried hot red chiles
>1 tablespoon chopped fresh cilantro (coriander)
>1½ cups regular-strength chicken broth
>1 pound rockfish fillets (*each ½ to ¾ inch thick*)
>4 flour tortillas (*each about 8 inches in diameter*)
>About 3 cups shredded iceberg lettuce
>About ⅔ cup sour cream

Prepare Salsa Fresca; cover and refrigerate.

In a 7- by 11-inch microwave-safe baking dish, stir together lemon juice, chiles, cilantro, and broth.

Rinse fish, pat dry, and place in dish, positioning thickest parts toward outside of dish. Cover and microwave on **HIGH (100%)** for 2 minutes. Turn fish over, cover, and microwave on **HIGH (100%)** for 2 minutes; let stand, covered, for 3 minutes. Fish should be just slightly translucent or wet inside; cut in thickest part to test. Lift fish to a warm serving dish; break into chunks. Reserve poaching liquid for other uses, if desired.

Moisten each tortilla with a little water. Stack tortillas on a plate, cover, and microwave on **HIGH (100%)** for 40 to 50 seconds or until hot.

To serve, spoon fish down center of each tortilla; top with Salsa Fresca, lettuce, and sour cream. Roll up and eat out of hand. Makes 4 servings.

Salsa Fresca. In a small bowl, stir together 1 large ripe **tomato,** diced; ¼ cup *each* chopped **onion** and chopped **fresh cilantro** (coriander); and 1 tablespoon *each* **lime juice** and seeded, diced **fresh jalapeño chile.** Season to taste with **salt.**

Per serving: 335 calories, 28 g protein, 31 g carbohydrates, 11 g total fat, 57 mg cholesterol, 677 mg sodium

STEAMED FISH & CLAMS IN BLACK BEAN SAUCE

Preparation time: About 15 minutes
Microwaving time: 8 to 10 minutes
Standing time: 2 minutes

The fermented black beans you need for this recipe are available in small jars or plastic bags in Asian markets and well-stocked supermarkets; you may see them labeled as salted or preserved black beans (*dow see*). If stored tightly covered in the refrigerator, they'll keep almost indefinitely.

- 1 **pound rockfish or lingcod fillets** (*each about 1 inch thick*)
- 1½ **tablespoons fermented black beans, rinsed, drained, and finely chopped**
- 2 **cloves garlic, minced or pressed**
- 1 **tablespoon** *each* **soy sauce and dry sherry**
- 3 **thin, quarter-size slices fresh ginger**
- 2 **green onions (including tops)**
- 12 **small hard-shell clams in shell, suitable for steaming, scrubbed**
- 2 **tablespoons salad oil**
   Fresh cilantro (coriander) sprigs

Rinse fish, pat dry, and place in a 7- by 11-inch microwave-safe baking dish. Combine beans, garlic, soy, and sherry; drizzle evenly over fish, then top with ginger. Cut 1 onion into thirds and place over ginger. Cut remaining onion into 2-inch lengths, then cut into thin shreds; set aside for garnish. Arrange clams around fish.

Cover and microwave on **HIGH (100%)** for 6 to 8 minutes, giving dish a quarter-turn every 2 minutes. Let stand, covered, for 2 minutes. Fish should be just slightly translucent or wet inside; cut in thickest part to test. If clams open before fish is done, remove clams and continue cooking fish a little longer; then return clams and juices to baking dish. Remove and discard ginger slices and onion pieces; sprinkle fish with reserved onion shreds.

Pour oil into a 1-cup glass measure; microwave, uncovered, on **HIGH (100%)** for 2 minutes or until very hot. Pour oil over fish and garnish with cilantro. Makes 3 servings.

Per serving: 286 calories, 37 g protein, 5 g carbohydrates, 12 g total fat, 73 mg cholesterol, 687 mg sodium

CLAM PILAF FOR TWO

Preparation time: About 15 minutes
Microwaving time: 19 to 26 minutes

Seafood and rice are classic partners. In this case, tender steamed clams pair up with a turmeric-seasoned pilaf that's bright with parsley and cherry tomato halves.

- 1 **clove garlic, minced or pressed**
- ¼ **teaspoon ground turmeric**
- ⅔ **cup long-grain white rice**
- 2 **tablespoons finely chopped parsley**
- ½ **cup cherry tomatoes, cut into halves**
- ⅔ **cup dry white wine**
   About ⅔ cup bottled clam juice or regular-strength chicken broth
- 24 **small hard-shell clams in shell, suitable for steaming, scrubbed**

In a 9-inch square microwave-safe baking dish, combine garlic, turmeric, rice, parsley, tomatoes, wine, and ⅔ cup of the clam juice. Cover and microwave on **HIGH (100%)** for 15 to 20 minutes or until rice is tender to bite and liquid has been absorbed; stir 3 or 4 times and add more clam juice if needed to keep rice moist.

Arrange clams on top of rice mixture. Cover and microwave on **HIGH (100%)** for 4 to 6 minutes or until clams open. Makes 2 servings.

Per serving: 319 calories, 19 g protein, 55 g carbohydrates, 1 g total fat, 37 mg cholesterol, 244 mg sodium

Topped with a cluster of Italian parsley and surrounded with lemon wedges, a platter of Butter-basted Crab (recipe on facing page) awaits hungry diners. Complete the finger-food feast with lots of crusty bread—and be sure to have big napkins on hand!

Pictured on facing page

BUTTER-BASTED CRAB

✳   ✳   ✳   ✳   ✳   ✳   ✳

Preparation time: 5 to 10 minutes
Microwaving time: 6 to 7 minutes

A lemon-butter baste sparked with soy and hot peppers flavors sweet, succulent crab. Serve crusty bread, a green salad, and dry white wine alongside; offer a fresh fruit sorbet for dessert.

- ½ cup (¼ lb.) butter or margarine
- ½ teaspoon grated lemon peel
- 6 tablespoons lemon juice
- 2 tablespoons thinly sliced green onion (including top)
- 2 teaspoons *each* minced parsley and soy sauce
  Liquid hot pepper seasoning
- 2 large cooked Dungeness or other hard-shell crabs (about 2 lbs. *each*), cleaned and cracked
  Lemon or lime wedges

Place butter in a 1-cup glass measure; microwave, uncovered, on **HIGH (100%)** for about 1 minute or until melted. Stir in lemon peel, lemon juice, onion, parsley, and soy; season to taste with hot pepper seasoning. Microwave, uncovered, on **HIGH (100%)** for 1 minute or until mixture is bubbly. Cover and set aside.

Rinse crabs, drain well, and arrange in an even layer in a 9- by 13-inch microwave-safe baking dish; brush with butter mixture. Cover and microwave on **HIGH (100%)** for 4 to 5 minutes or until hot through, brushing several times with remaining butter mixture and pan juices. Serve with lemon wedges. Makes 4 servings.

Per serving: 304 calories, 19 g protein, 3 g carbohydrates, 24 g total fat, 126 mg cholesterol, 732 mg sodium

TURBOT & CRAB CASSEROLE

✳   ✳   ✳   ✳   ✳   ✳   ✳

Preparation time: 20 to 25 minutes
Microwaving time: 16 to 19 minutes
Standing time: 2 minutes

Greenland turbot fillets are generally available in supermarkets for a moderate price. Because the cooked fish resembles crab in flavor and texture, it's a good extender for the more expensive seafood.

- 1 pound Greenland turbot fillets (thawed if frozen)
- 2 tablespoons butter or margarine
- ¾ cup thinly sliced celery
- ¼ pound mushrooms, sliced
- ½ small red bell pepper, seeded and chopped
- 2½ tablespoons all-purpose flour
- ¾ cup milk
- 3 tablespoons dry sherry
- ½ teaspoon dry savory leaves
- 1 teaspoon Dijon mustard
- ¼ teaspoon liquid hot pepper seasoning
- ⅛ teaspoon pepper
- ¼ pound crabmeat
- ½ cup sliced water chestnuts
- 3 tablespoons freshly grated Parmesan cheese
  Chopped parsley

Arrange turbot fillets in a 7- by 11-inch microwave-safe baking dish, positioning thickest parts toward outside of dish. Cover and microwave on **HIGH (100%)** for 4 to 6 minutes, turning fish over every 2 minutes. Let stand, covered, for 2 minutes. Fish should be just slightly translucent or wet inside; cut in thickest part to test. Lift out fish; drain well and break into bite-size pieces. Set aside.

Wipe out baking dish, then add butter, celery, mushrooms, and bell pepper. Cover and microwave on **HIGH (100%)** for 5 minutes or until mushrooms are limp, stirring every 1½ minutes. Blend in flour; microwave, uncovered, on **HIGH (100%)** for 1 minute or until bubbly. Gradually stir in milk and microwave, uncovered, on **HIGH (100%)** for 3 minutes or until sauce is thickened, stirring every 45 seconds. Stir in sherry, savory, mustard, hot pepper seasoning, pepper, crab, water chestnuts, and turbot.

Cover and microwave on **HIGH (100%)** for 2 to 3 minutes. Uncover and sprinkle with cheese. Microwave, uncovered, on **HIGH (100%)** for 1 minute or until hot through. Garnish with parsley. Makes 4 servings.

Per serving: 394 calories, 27 g protein, 14 g carbohydrates, 25 g total fat, 106 mg cholesterol, 406 mg sodium

GARLIC OYSTERS ON TOAST

Preparation time: About 10 minutes
Microwaving time: About 6 minutes
Standing time: 2 minutes

A garlic-butter bath and a brief "zap" in the microwave are all that's needed to transform a jar of shucked oysters into a memorable entrée. Serve the juicy shellfish on toast, crowned with cheese.

- ¼ cup butter or margarine
- 2 cloves garlic, minced or pressed
- 4 slices day-old French bread, toasted
- 1 jar (10 oz.) small shucked oysters
- 2 tablespoons thinly sliced green onion (including top)
- ¾ cup shredded jack cheese
  Chopped parsley

Place butter and garlic in an 8-inch square microwave-safe baking dish. Microwave, uncovered, on **HIGH (100%)** for about 45 seconds or until butter is melted. Lightly brush garlic butter over one side of each slice of toast; arrange toast, buttered side up, on a microwave-safe platter. Set aside.

Add oysters and their liquid to baking dish. Microwave, uncovered, on **HIGH (100%)** for 3 minutes or until oysters are heated through, stirring after 1½ minutes.

With a slotted spoon, arrange oysters on toast; add onion to juices in dish and set aside. Evenly sprinkle cheese over oysters. Microwave, uncovered, on **HIGH (100%)** for about 2 minutes or until cheese is melted, giving dish a half-turn after 1 minute. Let stand, uncovered, for 2 minutes.

Sprinkle oysters and cheese with parsley. Pour juices from baking dish into a small serving bowl; pass at the table to spoon over individual portions. Makes 2 servings.

Per serving: 669 calories, 27 g protein, 46 g carbohydrates, 41 g total fat, 179 mg cholesterol, 1,028 mg sodium

SCALLOPS WITH PEA PODS

Preparation time: About 15 minutes
Marinating time: 30 minutes
Microwaving time: 6 minutes
Standing time: 4 minutes

Scallops and fresh shiitake mushrooms are marinated in teriyaki sauce, then briefly cooked and served over bright green pea pods.

- 1 green onion (including top)
- 3 ounces fresh shiitake mushrooms
- ¾ pound scallops, rinsed well, drained, and cut into bite-size pieces
- 3 thin, quarter-size slices fresh ginger
- 5 teaspoons salad oil
- 4 teaspoons soy sauce
- 2 teaspoons dry sherry
- ½ pound Chinese pea pods (also called snow or sugar peas), ends and strings removed

Cut onion lengthwise into thin strips, then crosswise into 1-inch pieces. Reserve some of the onion slivers for garnish; place remainder in a shallow 1½-quart microwave-safe baking dish. Trim and discard tough stems of mushrooms; cut caps into thin strips. Add mushrooms to onion in baking dish along with scallops and ginger. Stir together oil, soy, and sherry; pour over scallop mixture and let marinate at room temperature for 30 minutes, stirring several times.

Spread scallop mixture out in an even layer. Cover and microwave on **HIGH (100%)** for 3 minutes, stirring after 2 minutes. Let stand, covered, for 4 minutes. Scallops should be opaque throughout; cut to test.

While scallops are standing, rinse pea pods; then place pea pods, with the water that clings to them, in a 1-quart microwave-safe baking dish. Cover and microwave on **HIGH (100%)** for 3 minutes or until tender-crisp to bite, stirring after 2 minutes. Transfer pea pods to a serving dish. Discard ginger, then spoon scallop mixture over pea pods. Garnish with reserved onion slivers. Makes 2 servings.

Per serving: 321 calories, 33 g protein, 17 g carbohydrates, 13 g total fat, 56 mg cholesterol, 969 mg sodium

QUICK & EASY
GRAIN
DISHES

A microwave can cook some grains in just half the usual time—but speed isn't the only advantage that microwaving offers. Microwaved polenta has a lighter, creamier texture, and it doesn't spatter or require constant stirring; barley becomes tender, yet retains its distinctly nutty flavor; and cracked wheat quickly fluffs into separate, moist little nuggets. And as a bonus, these grains can cook right in the serving bowl.

When you plan to serve one of the following grains as a side dish with a microwave entrée, start the grain of your choice first; while it stands, you can proceed with the main course.

PRESTO POLENTA

Preparation time: 2 to 3 minutes
Microwaving time: 12 to 13 minutes
Standing time: 8 to 10 minutes

Simple peasant food, polenta provides the perfect foil for spicy Italian dishes. Offer it as a side dish, embellished with butter and Parmesan cheese; or serve it as you would pasta, topped with your favorite meat or tomato sauce.

Polenta also makes a good breakfast. Once you've cooked it, pack it into a loaf pan; let cool, then cover and refrigerate until thoroughly chilled. Slice the polenta ½ inch thick, brown the slices in butter, and serve with maple syrup.

- 1 **cup polenta (Italian-style cornmeal) or yellow cornmeal**
- 3 **tablespoons butter or margarine**
- 1 **can (14½ oz.) regular-strength chicken broth**
- 1¾ **cups water**
  Grated Parmesan cheese
  Salt and pepper

In a 2½- to 3-quart microwave-safe casserole, combine polenta and 1 tablespoon of the butter. Stir in broth and water. Cover; microwave on **HIGH (100%)** for 12 to 13 minutes, stirring every 5 minutes. Let stand, covered, for 8 to 10 minutes or until polenta is thick and all liquid has been absorbed. Spoon into a serving dish. Dot with remaining 2 tablespoons butter and stir until butter is melted; then sprinkle with cheese. Season to taste with salt and pepper. Makes 4 to 6 servings.

Per serving: 171 calories, 3 g protein, 22 g carbohydrates, 8 g total fat, 19 mg cholesterol, 428 mg sodium

IN-A-HURRY BARLEY

Preparation time: 2 to 3 minutes
Microwaving time: 15 minutes
Standing time: 10 to 15 minutes

Chewy, nutty-tasting barley offers a delicious change of pace from steamed rice. Serve it plain as a side dish, top it with curried chicken or lamb, or add it to a meaty soup or stew for a hearty one-dish meal.

- 1 **cup pearl barley**
- 2 **cups water**
  Salt

Sort through barley and discard any debris. Rinse and drain barley; then place in a 2-quart microwave-safe casserole and stir in water. Cover and microwave on **HIGH (100%)** for 15 minutes, stirring every 5 minutes. Let stand, covered, for 10 to 15 minutes or until barley is tender to bite and all liquid has been absorbed. Season to taste with salt. Makes 4 servings.

Per serving: 172 calories, 5 g protein, 36 g carbohydrates, .5 g total fat, 0 mg cholesterol, 4 mg sodium

QUICK CRACKED WHEAT

Preparation time: 3 to 5 minutes
Microwaving time: About 9 minutes
Standing time: 5 minutes

This easy pilaf complements any simply cooked entrée—barbecued lamb or beef, roast chicken, poached fish. For a fancier version, you might sauté some sliced mushrooms in the butter before you add the wheat, or stir in diced pimento or thawed frozen peas along with the green onions.

- 2 **tablespoons butter or margarine**
- 1 **cup cracked wheat (bulgur)**
- 1 **can (14½ oz.) regular-strength chicken broth**
- ¼ **cup thinly sliced green onions (including tops)**

Place butter in a 2-quart microwave-safe casserole. Microwave, uncovered, on **HIGH (100%)** for about 35 seconds or until melted. Add cracked wheat and stir to coat thoroughly with butter; then stir in broth. Cover and microwave on **HIGH (100%)** for 8 minutes, stirring after 4 minutes. Stir in onions, cover, and let stand for 5 minutes or until wheat is tender to bite and all liquid has been absorbed. Fluff wheat with a fork; then serve. Makes 4 servings.

Per serving: 222 calories, 5 g protein, 36 g carbohydrates, 7 g total fat, 16 mg cholesterol, 508 mg sodium

CREAMY PASTA WITH SCALLOPS & SUN-DRIED TOMATOES

❋   ❋   ❋   ❋   ❋   ❋   ❋

Preparation time: 15 minutes
Microwaving time: 10 to 13 minutes
Standing time: 3 minutes

Looking for a special pasta sauce for your next dinner party? Try this outstanding combination of slivered sun-dried tomatoes and meaty sea scallops in a basil-seasoned cream sauce.

⅓ **cup dried tomatoes packed in oil**
1 **pound sea scallops**
1 **clove garlic, minced or pressed**
¼ **cup thinly sliced green onions (including tops)**
1½ **tablespoons chopped fresh basil leaves or 1 teaspoon dry basil leaves**
¼ **teaspoon ground white pepper**
½ **cup *each* regular-strength chicken broth and whipping cream**
⅓ **cup dry vermouth**
1 **tablespoon cornstarch blended with 1 tablespoon water**
8 **to 10 ounces dry wide egg noodles**
   Fresh basil sprigs (optional)
   Freshly grated Parmesan cheese

Sliver tomatoes and set aside; reserve oil. Rinse scallops well, cut in half horizontally, and pat dry.

Pour 1 tablespoon of the reserved tomato oil into a 9- or 10-inch square microwave-safe baking dish. Stir in garlic and scallops. Cover and microwave on **HIGH (100%)** for 3 minutes, stirring after 1½ minutes. Let stand, covered, for 3 minutes. Scallops should be opaque throughout; cut to test. Lift scallops from dish and set aside.

To dish, add slivered tomatoes, onions, basil leaves, white pepper, broth, cream, vermouth, and cornstarch mixture; stir to blend. Microwave, uncovered, on **HIGH (100%)** for 6 to 8 minutes or until mixture is bubbly and thickened, stirring every minute.

Meanwhile, cook noodles according to package directions; drain well, pour into a warm serving dish, and keep warm.

Return scallops to cream mixture and microwave, uncovered, on **HIGH (100%)** for 1 to 2 minutes or until scallops are heated through. Pour scallop mixture over noodles; garnish with basil sprigs, if desired. Pass cheese at the table to sprinkle over individual servings. Makes 4 servings.

Per serving: 522 calories, 29 g protein, 57 g carbohydrates, 19 g total fat, 131 mg cholesterol, 749 mg sodium

SCALLOPS & SHRIMP IN BÉARNAISE CREAM

❋   ❋   ❋   ❋   ❋   ❋   ❋

Preparation time: 20 minutes
Microwaving time: 15 to 18 minutes
Standing time: 2 minutes

The moist, tender textures and delicate flavors of scallops and shrimp are enhanced by this tarragon-seasoned cream sauce.

1 **pound sea scallops**
2 **tablespoons butter or margarine**
½ **pound medium-large raw shrimp (31 to 35 per lb.), shelled and deveined**
⅓ **cup finely chopped shallots**
½ **cup tarragon wine vinegar or white wine vinegar**
¼ **teaspoon dry tarragon**
1 **tablespoon Dijon mustard**
½ **cup whipping cream**
   Salt and ground white pepper

Rinse scallops well; cut in half horizontally, pat dry, and place in a 3-quart microwave-safe casserole along with butter and shrimp. Cover and microwave on **HIGH (100%)** for 5 to 6 minutes, stirring after 3 minutes; let stand, covered, for 2 minutes. Scallops and shrimp should be opaque throughout; cut to test. Using a slotted spoon, transfer seafood to a bowl; then cover and keep warm.

To casserole, add shallots, vinegar, tarragon, mustard, and cream. Microwave, uncovered, on **HIGH (100%)** for 10 to 12 minutes or until liquid is reduced to about ¾ cup; stir after 5 minutes. Stir in seafood and season to taste with salt and white pepper. Makes 4 servings.

Per serving: 307 calories, 30 g protein, 9 g carbohydrates, 17 g total fat, 157 mg cholesterol, 435 mg sodium

*Rich flavor and lovely looks make Creamy Pasta with Scallops &
Sun-dried Tomatoes (recipe on facing page) just right for a special meal.
Sweet scallops are cloaked in a creamy wine sauce accented with
strips of dried tomato, then served over tender broad noodles.*

COOKING
DINNER
FOR ONE

When it's dinner for one, put your microwave to work and cook an attractive meal right on your plate.

Pictured on page 2
SMOKED PORK CHOP SUPPER

* * * * *

Preparation time: 5 to 10 minutes
Microwaving time: About 4 minutes

- **Mustard Sauce (recipe follows)**
- 4 **to 6 dried apricots**
- 2 **or 3 pattypan squash (each about 2 inches in diameter)**
- 1 **smoked pork chop (about 7 oz.), cut ¾ inch thick**
- 1 **large or 2 small bran muffins**
- 1 **to 2 teaspoons butter or margarine**

Prepare Mustard Sauce. Place apricots in center of a microwave-safe dinner plate; spoon sauce over them. Cover and microwave on **HIGH (100%)** for 45 seconds or until hot. Meanwhile, rinse squash and trim ends; then cut each squash in half through trimmed ends.

Set pork chop on plate and spoon apricots and sauce over top. Place squash alongside. Cover and microwave on **HIGH (100%)** for 2½ to 3 minutes or until squash is tender-crisp when pierced, giving plate a half-turn after 1½ minutes.

Remove plate from oven. To heat muffin, microwave, uncovered, on **HIGH (100%)** for 10 to 20 seconds. Set muffin on plate; top with butter. Makes 1 serving.

Mustard Sauce. Mix 1 tablespoon *each* **Dijon mustard** and **honey** with ⅛ teaspoon **ground ginger.**

Per serving: 620 calories, 29 g protein, 77 g carbohydrates, 25 g total fat, 142 mg cholesterol, 2,279 mg sodium

SALMON & CUCUMBER PLATE

* * * * *

Preparation time: About 10 minutes
Microwaving time: 9 to 12 minutes

- 3 **small red thin-skinned potatoes (each about 1½ inches in diameter), scrubbed**
- 1 **tablespoon butter or margarine**
- 1 **large salmon steak (10 oz.)**
- ½ **teaspoon prepared horseradish**
- ¼ **to ½ cucumber, peeled and cut into julienne strips**
- **Dry dill weed**

Pierce each potato in several places to prevent bursting; place on a microwave-safe dinner plate and dot with butter. Cover and microwave on **HIGH (100%)** for 4 to 6 minutes or until potatoes are tender throughout when pierced.

Rinse fish and pat dry. Place fish next to potatoes on plate; cover and microwave on **HIGH (100%)** for 4 to 5 minutes, giving fish a half-turn after 2 minutes. Turn fish over; spread with horseradish. Then arrange cucumber on plate, turning to coat with juices. Sprinkle potatoes lightly with dill. Cover; microwave on **HIGH (100%)** for 40 to 50 more seconds or until cucumber is heated through. Fish should be just slightly translucent or wet inside; cut in thickest part to test. Makes 1 serving.

Per serving: 631 calories, 60 g protein, 28 g carbohydrates, 30 g total fat, 187 mg cholesterol, 260 mg sodium

PIZZA-TOPPED ONION WITH SAUSAGE

* * * * *

Preparation time: 5 to 8 minutes
Microwaving time: 9 to 10 minutes

- 1 **medium-size onion, peeled and cut in half lengthwise**
- ¼ **pound green beans, stem ends snapped off**
- 1 **garlic frankfurter or other fully cooked sausage (4 to 5 oz.)**
- 2 **tablespoons tomato paste**
- 2 **slices mozzarella cheese (about 1 oz. each)**
- 2 **tablespoons grated Parmesan cheese**
- ½ **teaspoon dry oregano leaves**
- **Spicy brown mustard**

Place onion halves, cut sides up, in center of a microwave-safe dinner plate; cover and microwave on **HIGH (100%)** for 5 to 6 minutes or until onion is tender when pierced.

Rinse beans and arrange alongside onion. Cover and microwave on **HIGH (100%)** for 2 minutes or until beans turn bright green.

Slit sausage lengthwise, cutting almost all the way through; open out flat. Arrange on plate next to onion halves. Cover and microwave on **HIGH (100%)** for about 1 minute or until sausage is heated through.

Spread 1 tablespoon of the tomato paste on top of each onion half. Top each with a slice of mozzarella cheese and 1 tablespoon of the Parmesan cheese. Then sprinkle each with ¼ teaspoon of the oregano. Cover and microwave on **HIGH (100%)** for 40 to 45 seconds or just until cheese is melted. Serve mustard on the side to spread on sausage. Makes 1 serving.

Per serving: 633 calories, 32 g protein, 24 g carbohydrates, 46 g total fat, 119 mg cholesterol, 1,677 mg sodium

SHRIMP & CABBAGE, ASIAN STYLE

Preparation time: 15 to 20 minutes
Microwaving time: 18 to 19 minutes
Standing time: 2 minutes

A microwave browning dish works well for this simple one-dish meal. Offer hot cooked brown rice on the side and chilled canned lychees for dessert.

  Cooking Sauce (recipe follows)
1 package (8 oz.) brown-and-serve sausages
1 small onion, thinly sliced
1 clove garlic, minced or pressed
1 can (about 8 oz.) bamboo shoots, drained
3 to 4 cups finely shredded green cabbage
½ pound tiny cooked and shelled shrimp
  Thinly sliced green onions (including tops)

Prepare Cooking Sauce; set aside.

Preheat a 2- to 2½-quart or 10-inch square microwave browning dish on **HIGH (100%)** for 4½ minutes. Using oven mitts, carefully remove dish to a heatproof surface. Add sausages, cover, and microwave on **HIGH (100%)** for 2 minutes, stirring every 30 seconds. Lift out sausages, cut each into thirds, and set aside.

Discard all but 1 tablespoon of the drippings from browning dish; add sliced onion and garlic. Cover and microwave on **HIGH (100%)** for 5 minutes or until onion is soft, stirring after 2½ minutes. Stir in bamboo shoots and cabbage. Cover and microwave on **HIGH (100%)** for 3 minutes, stirring after 1½ minutes. Stir in shrimp, sausages, and Cooking Sauce. Microwave, uncovered, on **HIGH (100%)** for 3 to 4 minutes or until sauce is thickened and bubbly, stirring every minute. Let stand, covered, for 2 minutes. Sprinkle with green onions, then serve. Makes 3 servings.

Cooking Sauce. Stir together 3 tablespoons **soy sauce,** 2 tablespoons **dry sherry,** ¾ teaspoon *each* **sugar** and **ground ginger,** ⅛ teaspoon **pepper,** and 1 tablespoon **cornstarch.**

Per serving: 308 calories, 24 g protein, 14 g carbohydrates, 17 g total fat, 173 mg cholesterol, 1,521 mg sodium

FLASH-IN-THE-PAN SHRIMP & SPINACH

Preparation time: About 25 minutes
Microwaving time: 12 to 13 minutes
Standing time: About 4 minutes

Once you've readied all the ingredients, you can whip up this main dish in a flash. Sweet seedless grapes deliciously accent the juicy shrimp and fresh spinach.

  About ¾ pound spinach, rinsed well
1 pound medium-size raw shrimp (35 to 45 per lb.), shelled and deveined
3 green onions (including tops), thinly sliced
½ cup whipping cream
2 tablespoons Dijon mustard
½ teaspoon grated orange peel
⅛ teaspoon ground nutmeg
1½ cups seedless grapes (½ to ¾ lb.)
  Salt

Remove and discard stems and any yellow or wilted leaves from spinach; then pat spinach dry and set aside.

Combine shrimp and onions in a 3- to 3½-quart microwave-safe casserole. Cover and microwave on **HIGH (100%)** for 4 minutes, stirring after 2 minutes. Let stand, covered, for 2 minutes. Shrimp should be opaque throughout; cut to test. With a slotted spoon, transfer shrimp mixture to a bowl; cover and set aside.

To casserole, add cream, mustard, orange peel, and nutmeg. Stir to blend well. Microwave, uncovered, on **HIGH (100%)** for 5 to 6 minutes or until sauce is thickened, stirring after 3 minutes. Stir in grapes and shrimp mixture; cover and microwave on **HIGH (100%)** for 3 minutes. Lightly mix in spinach, cover, and let stand for about 2 minutes to wilt and heat spinach. Season to taste with salt; then serve immediately. Makes 4 servings.

Per serving: 251 calories, 22 g protein, 16 g carbohydrates, 12 g total fat, 173 mg cholesterol, 421 mg sodium

Marinated in lemon, wine, and garlic, tender Chicken Breasts with Anchovies & Red Peppers (recipe on page 76) are a colorful, savory choice for an Italian-style meal. You might serve the chicken on a bed of buttered green fettuccine.

Poultry

As the recipes in this chapter attest, ever-popular poultry takes beautifully to microwaving. Budget-wise chicken choices include entrées made with boneless breasts or whole legs; to save calories, we often remove the skin and flavor the meat with a sauce or marinade. You'll also find casseroles based on meaty drumsticks and cooked chicken chunks. Besides chicken, we offer turkey dishes and game hen recipes that are just right for quick company fare. For tips on microwaving poultry, see the chart on page 77.

Pictured on page 74

CHICKEN BREASTS WITH ANCHOVIES & RED PEPPERS

✳ ✳ ✳ ✳ ✳ ✳ ✳

Preparation time: 5 to 10 minutes
Marinating time: At least 30 minutes
Microwaving time: About 10 minutes
Standing time: 2 minutes

Sporting the bright red, white, and green colors of Italy's national flag, this piquant-salty dish proves just how easy it can be to microwave with an Italian flair.

    3   whole chicken breasts (about 1 lb. *each*), skinned, boned, and split
    ¼   cup dry vermouth
    2   tablespoons olive oil
    1   tablespoon lemon juice
    ½   teaspoon grated lemon peel
    1   clove garlic, minced or pressed
    1   small red bell pepper, seeded and cut into thin strips
    6   canned flat anchovy fillets, drained and coarsely chopped
    1   teaspoon capers, drained
    1   tablespoon chopped parsley
        Lemon wedges (optional)

Rinse chicken and pat dry. In a wide, shallow bowl, stir together vermouth, oil, lemon juice, lemon peel, and garlic. Add chicken and turn to coat; then cover and refrigerate for at least 30 minutes or up to 4 hours. Lift chicken from marinade and reserve marinade.

In a 10- to 11-inch microwave-safe baking dish, arrange chicken in a single layer, positioning thickest parts of breasts toward outside of dish. Cover and microwave on **HIGH (100%)** for about 6 minutes, giving dish a quarter-turn every 1½ minutes. Let stand, covered, for 2 minutes. Chicken should no longer be pink in thickest part; cut to test. Lift chicken from dish and set aside.

Add marinade and bell pepper to dish. Microwave, uncovered, on **HIGH (100%)** for 3 minutes or until pepper is tender-crisp to bite, stirring every minute.

Return chicken to dish, arranging it in a single layer; spoon sauce and peppers up over chicken. Sprinkle with anchovies and capers. Microwave, uncovered, on **HIGH (100%)** for 1 minute or until heated through. Sprinkle with parsley and garnish with lemon wedges, if desired. Makes 6 servings.

Per serving: 219 calories, 35 g protein, 2 g carbohydrates, 7 g total fat, 88 mg cholesterol, 257 mg sodium

TERIYAKI GINGER CHICKEN BREASTS

✳ ✳ ✳ ✳ ✳ ✳ ✳

Preparation time: About 5 minutes
Marinating time: 30 minutes to 1 hour
Microwaving time: 2½ minutes
Standing time: 1 minute

If you enjoy Asian flavors, you'll want to try this easy entrée for two. Just soak boneless chicken breasts in a soy-ginger marinade, then microwave until tender. Complete the meal with bright green snow peas and buttered winter squash.

    1   large whole chicken breast (about 1¼ lbs.), skinned, boned, and split
    1½ tablespoons soy sauce
    1   tablespoon *each* sugar and dry sherry
    ½   teaspoon grated fresh ginger
    1   clove garlic, minced or pressed
        Fresh cilantro (coriander) sprigs (optional)

Rinse chicken and pat dry. In a 9-inch square microwave-safe baking dish, stir together soy, sugar, sherry, ginger, and garlic. Add chicken and turn to coat with marinade. Cover and let stand at room temperature for 30 minutes to 1 hour, turning chicken over occasionally.

Drain marinade from chicken and reserve. Arrange chicken with thickest parts toward outside of dish; cover and microwave on **HIGH (100%)** for 1½ minutes. Give dish a half-turn. Brush chicken with marinade, cover, and microwave on **HIGH (100%)** for 1 minute. Let stand, covered, for 1 minute. Chicken should no longer be pink in thickest part; cut to test. Garnish with cilantro, if desired. Makes 2 servings.

Per serving: 220 calories, 39 g protein, 9 g carbohydrates, 2 g total fat, 96 mg cholesterol, 880 mg sodium

✳ POULTRY COOKING CHART ✳

CAUTION: To prevent overcooking, use shortest cooking time. Let poultry stand for recommended time, then test for doneness as directed. If necessary, continue to microwave in 1-minute increments. To cover poultry for cooking, you may use heavy-duty plastic wrap, the container lid, or (to cover loosely) wax paper.

POULTRY	PREPARATION	COOKING TIME (CT) STANDING TIME (ST)
Frying chicken, whole (3–3½ lbs.)	If frozen, thaw completely. Remove giblets and neck. Rinse bird inside and out; pat dry. Rub skin with butter or margarine and paprika. Place bird, breast down, on a microwave-safe rack in a 7- by 11-inch microwave-safe baking dish. Cover.	CT: 6–7 minutes per lb. Microwave on **HIGH (100%).** Turn breast up halfway through cooking. ST: 5 minutes, loosely covered with foil. Meat near thighbone should no longer be pink; cut to test.
Frying chicken, cut up (3–3½ lbs.)	Rinse; pat dry. Arrange pieces, skin side down, in a 9- by 13-inch microwave-safe baking dish, positioning thickest parts toward outside of dish. Cover.	CT: 6–7 minutes per lb. Microwave on **HIGH (100%).** Turn skin side up halfway through cooking. If desired, uncover, discard liquid, and baste with barbecue sauce for last 10 minutes. ST: 3–5 minutes, covered (uncovered, if basted). Meat near thighbone should no longer be pink; cut to test.
Chicken legs, thighs attached (About 8 oz. *each*)	Rinse; pat dry. Arrange pieces, skin side down, in a 7- by 11-inch microwave-safe baking dish, positioning thighs toward outside of dish. Cover.	CT: 7 minutes per lb. Microwave on **HIGH (100%),** turning over halfway through cooking. ST: 3 minutes, covered. Meat near thighbone should no longer be pink; cut to test.
Chicken breast, split (1–1¼ lbs.)	Remove bones and skin. Rinse; pat dry. Place in a 9-inch square microwave-safe baking dish, positioning thickest parts toward outside of dish. Cover.	CT: 2½–3 minutes per lb. Microwave on **HIGH (100%),** giving dish ½ turn halfway through cooking. ST: 1 minute, covered. Meat should no longer be pink in thickest part; cut to test.
Turkey, whole (10–14 lbs.; we don't recommend microwaving a bird over 14 lbs.)	If frozen, thaw completely. Remove giblets and neck; rinse bird inside and out and pat dry. Secure neck skin to back with bamboo skewer. With string, tie legs together and wings to breast. Rub skin with butter or margarine and paprika. Place bird, breast down, in a 9- by 13-inch microwave-safe baking dish.	CT: 7–8 minutes per lb. Determine total cooking time; divide into 4 equal periods. Microwave on **HIGH (100%).** Position bird as follows: first period, breast down; second period, right wing down; third period, left wing down; fourth period, breast up. Discard juices each time bird is turned. At end of cooking time, a meat thermometer inserted in thickest part of thigh (not touching bone) should register 170°F. ST: 15 minutes, loosely covered with foil.
Turkey breast, half (3–3½ lbs.)	Remove bones and skin, if desired. Place in a 7- by 11-inch microwave-safe baking dish. Cover.	CT: 4–6 minutes per lb. Microwave on **HIGH (100%),** turning over halfway through cooking. ST: 5–7 minutes, covered. Meat should no longer be pink in thickest part; cut to test.
Turkey drumsticks (1–1¼ lbs. *each*)	Rinse; pat dry. Arrange in a 7- by 11-inch microwave-safe baking dish, positioning thickest parts toward outside of dish. Brush with melted butter or margarine. Cover.	CT: 20 minutes per lb. Determine total cooking time. Microwave on **HIGH (100%)** for 10 minutes. Turn legs over; microwave on **MEDIUM-LOW (30%)** for remaining time, turning legs over halfway through cooking. Discard juices in dish. ST: 15 minutes, covered. Meat near thighbone should no longer be pink; cut to test.
Rock Cornish game hens (1¼–1½ lbs. *each*)	Same as whole chicken. Leave legs free; bend wings akimbo. Place, breast down, on a microwave-safe rack in a 7- by 11-inch microwave-safe baking dish. Cover.	CT: 6 minutes per lb. Microwave on **HIGH (100%),** turning breast up halfway through cooking. ST: 5 minutes, loosely covered with foil. Meat near thighbone should no longer be pink; cut to test.

ORANGE-ALMOND CHICKEN

✳   ✳   ✳   ✳   ✳   ✳   ✳

Preparation time: 5 to 10 minutes
Microwaving time: 13 to 14 minutes

Dotted with raisins, bits of bell pepper, and mandarin orange segments, this breast of chicken dish makes a colorful entrée. Spoon it over rice, then top with crisp toasted almonds.

  2 **tablespoons slivered blanched almonds**
  2 **whole chicken breasts (about 1 lb.**
     ***each*), skinned, boned, and cut into**
     ¾- by 2-inch strips
     Garlic salt and pepper
  2 **teaspoons curry powder**
  2 **tablespoons salad oil**
  1 **can (11 oz.) mandarin oranges**
  2 **tablespoons *each* raisins and chopped**
     Major Grey's chutney
  1 **medium-size red or green bell pepper,**
     seeded and chopped
  1 **tablespoon cornstarch**
     Hot cooked rice

Spread almonds in a 2- to 2½-quart or 10-inch square microwave browning dish. Microwave, uncovered, on **HIGH (100%)** for 3 minutes or until nuts are golden, stirring every 20 seconds. Remove from dish and set aside.

Sprinkle chicken lightly with garlic salt and pepper; then sprinkle with curry powder. Return browning dish to microwave and preheat on **HIGH (100%)** for 3 minutes. Using oven mitts, remove dish to a heatproof surface. Add oil and tilt to coat bottom of dish; quickly add chicken in a single layer. Wait until sizzling stops; then cover and microwave on **HIGH (100%)** for 2½ minutes, stirring after 1½ minutes.

Drain oranges, reserving liquid. Set oranges aside. Combine raisins, chutney, bell pepper, and ¼ cup of the reserved liquid. Add to chicken in dish; stir to mix, then cover and microwave on **HIGH (100%)** for 2 minutes. Combine remaining orange liquid and cornstarch; stir into chicken mixture with the oranges. Microwave, uncovered, on **HIGH (100%)** for 2 to 3 minutes or until sauce is thick and clear, stirring every minute. Spoon chicken mixture over rice; garnish with toasted almonds. Makes 4 servings.

Per serving: 344 calories, 36 g protein, 26 g carbohydrates, 11 g total fat, 86 mg cholesterol, 120 mg sodium

Pictured on facing page

SWEET CHILI CHICKEN

✳   ✳   ✳   ✳   ✳   ✳   ✳

Preparation time: 3 to 5 minutes
Microwaving time: 18 minutes
Standing time: 3 to 5 minutes

For a great summer dinner, try tender whole chicken legs basted with a quick-to-fix sweet-sour barbecue sauce.

  4 **whole chicken legs, thighs attached**
     (about 2½ lbs. *total*), skinned
  ¾ **cup tomato-based chili sauce**
  1½ **tablespoons *each* white vinegar, firmly**
     packed brown sugar, and minced green
     onion (including top)
  ¾ **teaspoon *each* dry mustard and**
     Worcestershire

Rinse chicken and pat dry.

In a shallow 2- to 2½-quart microwave-safe baking dish, stir together chili sauce, vinegar, sugar, onion, mustard, and Worcestershire. Add chicken and turn to coat. Arrange chicken with thighs toward outside of dish. Cover and microwave on **HIGH (100%)** for 10 minutes, giving dish a half-turn after 5 minutes. Turn chicken to bring uncooked portions to outside of dish; spoon sauce over chicken. Microwave, uncovered, on **HIGH (100%)** for 8 minutes, giving dish a half-turn after 4 minutes. Let stand, uncovered, for 3 to 5 minutes. Meat near thighbone should no longer be pink; cut to test. Makes 4 servings.

Per serving: 271 calories, 34 g protein, 18 g carbohydrates, 6 g total fat, 130 mg cholesterol, 837 mg sodium

*It looks like a traditional treat from the barbecue— but Sweet Chili Chicken
(recipe on facing page) comes from the microwave, not the backyard grill.
Accompany the juicy chicken legs with old-fashioned picnic favorites: three-
bean salad, deviled eggs, and asssorted fresh fruit.*

INDIAN CHICKEN CURRY

✳   ✳   ✳   ✳   ✳   ✳   ✳

Preparation time: 10 to 15 minutes
Microwaving time: 19 to 21 minutes
Standing time: 3 minutes

Fragrant but mild, this bright curry sauce combines curry powder and ginger with bits of onion and sweet apple. Serve chicken and sauce with hot cooked rice and a trio of condiments.

    2 tablespoons butter or margarine
    ½ cup *each* chopped onion and finely
       chopped Golden Delicious apple
    2 tablespoons all-purpose flour
   2½ teaspoons curry powder
    ¼ teaspoon ground ginger
    1 teaspoon sugar
    ½ cup *each* milk and regular-strength
       chicken broth
    1 teaspoon lemon juice
    2 whole chicken legs, thighs attached
       (about 1¼ lbs. *total*), skinned
       About 1½ cups hot cooked rice
    2 tablespoons *each* salted roasted peanuts
       and raisins
    ½ banana, sliced

Place butter in a 9-inch square microwave-safe baking dish. Microwave, uncovered, on **HIGH (100%)** for about 35 seconds or until butter is melted. Add onion and apple; stir to coat with butter. Then microwave, uncovered, on **HIGH (100%)** for 5 minutes, stirring after 2½ minutes. Stir in flour, curry powder, ginger, and sugar. Microwave, uncovered, on **HIGH (100%)** for 1 minute or until bubbly. Gradually stir in milk and broth to make a smooth sauce. Stir in lemon juice.

Rinse chicken and pat dry; add to sauce and turn to coat. Arrange chicken with thighs toward outside of dish. Cover and microwave on **HIGH (100%)** for 7 minutes, giving dish a half-turn after 3½ minutes. Turn chicken to bring uncooked portions to outside of dish; spoon sauce over chicken. Cover and microwave on **HIGH (100%)** for 5 to 7 minutes, giving dish a half-turn after 3 minutes. Let stand, covered, for 3 minutes. Meat near thighbone should no longer be pink; cut to test.

To serve, mound half the rice on each of 2 dinner plates. Top each mound with a piece of chicken, half the sauce, and equal portions of peanuts, raisins, and banana slices. Makes 2 servings.

Per serving: 717 calories, 44 g protein, 79 g carbohydrates, 26 g total fat, 169 mg cholesterol, 619 mg sodium

GARLIC CHICKEN WITH GRAPES

✳   ✳   ✳   ✳   ✳   ✳   ✳

Preparation time: About 5 minutes
Microwaving time: About 26 minutes

Tart, snappy red grapes provide a refreshing contrast to the spicy soy-mustard seasoning that coats these chicken legs.

    4 whole chicken legs, thighs attached
       (about 2½ lbs. *total*)
    2 tablespoons butter or margarine, melted
    1 tablespoon sesame seeds
    2 tablespoons *each* Dijon mustard and soy
       sauce
    4 teaspoons *each* honey and white wine vinegar
    1 large clove garlic, minced or pressed
   1½ cups red or green seedless grapes (½ to ¾ lb.)

Rinse chicken and pat dry. Brush chicken evenly with butter, then sprinkle with sesame seeds.

Preheat a 2- to 2½-quart or 10-inch square microwave browning dish on **HIGH (100%)** for 4½ minutes. Using oven mitts, carefully remove dish to a heatproof surface. Quickly arrange chicken in dish, skin side down, with thighs toward outside; then wait until sizzling stops. Meanwhile, in a cup, blend together mustard, soy, honey, vinegar, and garlic.

Evenly spread half the mustard mixture over tops of chicken pieces. Cover and microwave on **HIGH (100%)** for 10 minutes, giving dish a half-turn after 5 minutes. Turn chicken pieces over, then rearrange to bring uncooked portions to outside of dish. Top with remaining mustard mixture. Microwave, uncovered, on **HIGH (100%)** for about 6 minutes, giving dish a half-turn after 3 minutes.

Sprinkle grapes around chicken. Microwave, uncovered, on **HIGH (100%)** for about 5 minutes or until grapes are heated through and meat near thighbone is no longer pink; cut to test. Makes 4 servings.

Per serving: 543 calories, 39 g protein, 23 g carbohydrates, 33 g total fat, 188 mg cholesterol, 964 mg sodium

SIMPLE
MICROWAVE
BREADS

Most breads don't fare too well in the microwave—but these three recipes were developed to turn out perfectly.

CHEWY WHEAT ROUNDS

Preparation time: 35 to 40 minutes
Rising time: About 2 hours
Microwaving time: 3 minutes per bread

1 package active dry yeast
¾ cup warm water (about 110°F)
2 cups whole wheat flour
¾ teaspoon salt
    About 2 tablespoons butter or margarine, melted

In a 1-cup measure, sprinkle yeast over warm water and let stand for 5 minutes. Measure 1¾ cups of the flour into a large bowl; stir in salt. Pour yeast mixture into flour and mix until well blended. Sprinkle remaining ¼ cup flour on a board; turn out dough onto board and knead for 3 to 5 minutes to form a soft dough.

Place dough in a lightly greased bowl; turn over to grease top. Cover and let rise in a warm place until doubled in bulk (about 2 hours). Punch dough down, turn out onto an unfloured board, and knead lightly. Divide dough into 6 equal portions. Shape each portion into a ball; cover and let rest for 15 minutes. Stretch and press each ball into a 6-inch circle; brush tops with melted butter.

To cook, place one round at a time on a microwave-safe rack in a microwave-safe baking dish. Microwave, uncovered, on **MEDIUM (50%)** for 3 minutes or until bread springs back when lightly touched. If necessary, wipe rack dry before baking next bread. Makes 6 breads.

Per bread: 170 calories, 6 g protein, 29 g carbohydrates, 5 g total fat, 10 mg cholesterol, 315 mg sodium

CHINESE FLOWER ROLLS

Preparation time: About 20 minutes
Rising time: About 30 minutes
Microwaving time: 2 minutes to thaw dough; 4 minutes to cook rolls
Standing time: About 3 minutes

1 loaf (1 lb.) frozen bread dough
    Salad oil

To thaw frozen bread dough, place it (unwrapped) in a 9-inch microwave-safe pie plate or baking dish. Brush loaf with oil. Microwave dough, uncovered, on **MEDIUM (50%)** for 2 minutes, turning loaf over after 1 minute; then let stand until soft (about 3 minutes).

Cut loaf into 16 equal pieces; shape each into a ball. Roll out each ball into a 3-inch round and brush it with oil. Fold rounds in half. Set aside in a warm place on a sheet of plastic wrap; cover rounds and let rise until doubled in bulk (about 30 minutes).

You can cook 4 rolls at a time. Place rolls slightly apart on pie plate; microwave, uncovered, on **HIGH (100%)** for 1 minute or until rolls feel fairly firm and look dry on the surface. Remove rolls from plate and turn upside down on a serving dish to let undersides dry slightly. Serve warm. Makes 16 rolls.

Per roll: 84 calories, 2 g protein, 13 g carbohydrates, 2 g total fat, 1 mg cholesterol, 137 mg sodium

MICRO-BAKE BRAN MUFFINS

Preparation time: 5 to 10 minutes
Microwaving time: 45 to 60 seconds per muffin
Standing time: 30 to 60 seconds per muffin

1½ cups whole bran cereal
½ cup boiling water
1 large egg
1 cup buttermilk
¼ cup salad oil
½ cup raisins
1¼ teaspoons baking soda
¼ teaspoon salt
½ cup sugar
1¼ cups all-purpose flour

In a large bowl, blend bran cereal with boiling water, stirring to moisten evenly. Let cool. Add egg, buttermilk, oil, and raisins; blend well. Combine baking soda, salt, sugar, and flour; stir flour mixture into bran mixture.

Bake muffins as soon as mixed; or refrigerate batter in a tightly covered container for up to 10 days, baking muffins at your convenience. Stir batter before using.

To bake, nest 2 paper baking cups, one inside the other (don't use foil-backed cups). Invert doubled cup and wrap a strip of tape around middle of outside cup. Turn doubled cup right side up; spoon in ¼ cup batter.

Microwave, uncovered, on **HIGH (100%)** for 45 to 60 seconds, giving cup a half-turn after 25 seconds. Muffin should look dry on top and spring back when lightly touched; it may feel moist but should not be sticky. Let stand for 30 to 60 seconds before eating. Makes 12 to 15 muffins.

Per muffin: 143 calories, 3 g protein, 26 g carbohydrates, 5 g total fat, 15 mg cholesterol, 204 mg sodium

Topped with two cheeses and garnished with buttery-smooth avocado slices, plump Chicken & Green Chile Enchiladas (recipe on facing page) are sure to satisfy. Offer plenty of iced tea for sipping alongside, and a platter of chilled melon wedges for dessert.

MUSTARD CHICKEN CHUNKS WITH VERMICELLI

✳ ✳ ✳ ✳ ✳ ✳ ✳

Preparation time: 5 to 10 minutes
Microwaving time: About 17 minutes

Boneless chicken thighs turn out moist and succulent when micro-braised with white wine, mustard, and herbs.

1½ pounds boneless chicken thighs, skinned
1½ tablespoons butter or margarine
  1 small clove garlic, minced or pressed
  1 teaspoon mustard seeds, coarsely crushed
  ¼ teaspoon dry tarragon
  ⅓ cup dry white wine
  2 teaspoons Dijon mustard
  ¼ cup sliced green onions (including tops)
  ½ cup sour cream
  8 to 10 ounces dry vermicelli or other thin pasta, cooked and drained (keep hot)

Rinse chicken and pat dry. Preheat a 2- to 2½-quart or 10-inch square microwave browning dish on

HIGH (100%) for 4½ minutes. Using oven mitts, carefully remove dish to a heatproof surface. Add butter; swirl dish to coat bottom with butter. Immediately add chicken thighs in a single layer. Wait until sizzling stops, then turn chicken over and sprinkle evenly with garlic, mustard seeds, and tarragon. Cover and microwave on HIGH (100%) for 5 minutes, giving dish a half-turn after 2½ minutes. Chicken should no longer be pink in center; cut to test. Lift out chicken and set aside.

Stir wine and mustard into liquid in dish. Microwave, uncovered, on HIGH (100%) for 5 minutes or until mixture comes to a boil and browns slightly at edges.

Return chicken to dish; stir in onions and sour cream. Microwave, uncovered, on MEDIUM (50%) for 2 minutes or until sauce is heated through, stirring after 1 minute. Serve over hot cooked vermicelli. Makes 4 servings.

Per serving: 549 calories, 43 g protein, 50 g carbohydrates, 18 g total fat, 166 mg cholesterol, 287 mg sodium

---

Pictured on facing page

CHICKEN & GREEN CHILE ENCHILADAS

✳ ✳ ✳ ✳ ✳ ✳ ✳

Preparation time: About 30 minutes
Microwaving time: 16 minutes
Standing time: 5 minutes

A creamy, cumin-flavored chicken filling is tucked inside these hearty enchiladas.

  1 tablespoon salad oil
  1 medium-size onion, thinly sliced
  ½ teaspoon ground cumin
  ¼ teaspoon dry oregano leaves
  ⅓ cup whipping cream
  1 can (4 oz.) diced green chiles
  3 cups diced cooked chicken (about a 3½-lb. frying chicken; see page 77 for directions for cooking chicken)
  1 small tomato, seeded and chopped
  2 cups (8 oz.) shredded jack cheese
  8 flour tortillas, *each* about 8 inches in diameter (make sure tortillas are soft and pliable)
  1 cup (4 oz.) shredded Cheddar cheese
  1 small ripe avocado (optional)
  4 whole radishes; or 8 cherry tomatoes, halved
    Fresh cilantro (coriander) sprigs
  ½ cup sour cream (optional)

Place oil in an 8- by 12-inch microwave-safe baking dish. Arrange onion slices evenly in oil; sprinkle with cumin and oregano. Microwave, uncovered, on HIGH (100%) for 5 minutes or until onion is soft, stirring after 2½ minutes. Add cream; microwave, uncovered, on HIGH (100%) for 3 minutes or until cream is hot and bubbly. Stir in chiles, chicken, chopped tomato, and 1 cup of the jack cheese.

Place tortillas on a flat surface; top equally with chicken filling. Clean baking dish used for filling; lightly grease dish. Roll up tortillas; place, seam side down, in a single layer in dish. Sprinkle with remaining 1 cup jack cheese, then with Cheddar cheese. Cover and microwave on MEDIUM-HIGH (70–80%) for 8 minutes, giving dish a half-turn after 4 minutes. Let stand, covered, for 5 minutes or until enchiladas in center are hot.

Pit, peel, and slice avocado (if used). Divide enchiladas among 4 plates. Garnish with avocado, radishes or cherry tomato halves, cilantro, and sour cream (if used). Makes 4 servings.

Per serving: 861 calories, 59 g protein, 53 g carbohydrates, 45 g total fat, 195 mg cholesterol, 1,171 mg sodium

FIVE-WAY CHICKEN BREASTS

Your microwave oven does a superb job of cooking chicken breasts to moist succulence in record time. We've developed a basic recipe that's a great centerpiece for a simple family dinner—and equally good as a base for other main dishes.

You can use our Micro-steamed Chicken Breasts in your own favorite entrées calling for cooked chicken, or try the four suggestions here: a savory chicken and rice casserole, a cool salad with fresh fruit, a creamy pasta dish flavored with sausage, and an easy adaptation of mu shu chicken.

MICRO-STEAMED CHICKEN BREASTS

Preparation time: 5 minutes
Marinating time: 30 minutes
Microwaving time: About 6 minutes
Standing time: 2 minutes

- ½ cup dry sherry
- 2 tablespoons soy sauce
- 1 teaspoon sugar
- ½ teaspoon ground ginger
- 1 clove garlic, minced or pressed
- 3 whole chicken breasts (about 1 lb. *each*), skinned, boned, and split

In a wide, shallow bowl, stir together sherry, soy, sugar, ginger, and garlic; add chicken and turn to coat. Cover and refrigerate for at least 30 minutes or up to 2 hours. Lift chicken from marinade; reserve marinade if you plan to make Mu Shu Chicken (recipe on facing page).

Arrange chicken breasts in a single layer in a shallow 10- to 12-inch microwave-safe baking dish or plate, positioning thickest parts toward outside of dish. Cover and microwave on **HIGH (100%)** for about 6 minutes, giving dish a

quarter-turn every 1½ minutes. Let stand, covered, for 2 minutes. Chicken should no longer be pink in thickest part; cut to test. Serve; or use in any of the following recipes. Makes 6 servings.

Per serving: 171 calories, 34 g protein, 2 g carbohydrates, 2 g total fat, 86 mg cholesterol, 268 mg sodium

CHICKEN & RICE BAKE

Preparation time: About 10 minutes
Microwaving time: About 28 minutes

- ½ pound andouille sausage or kielbasa (Polish sausage), sliced ¼ inch thick
- 1 clove garlic, minced or pressed
- 1 small onion, chopped
- 1 cup short-grain white rice (such as pearl)
- 1 jar (4 oz.) sliced pimentos, drained
- 1 can (6½ oz.) minced clams
- 1 can (14½ oz.) regular-strength chicken broth
  Micro-steamed Chicken Breasts (at left), cut crosswise into bite-size strips
- 2 green onions (including tops), thinly sliced
  Fresh cilantro (coriander) sprigs

Preheat a 2- to 2½-quart or 10-inch square microwave browning dish on **HIGH (100%)** for 4½ minutes. Using oven mitts, carefully remove dish to a heatproof surface. Add sausage slices and let brown for 2½ minutes, turn-

ing after 1 minute. Lift sausage from dish with a slotted spoon; set aside.

Add garlic and chopped onion to sausage drippings in dish, turning to coat. Microwave, uncovered, on **HIGH (100%)** for 5 minutes or until onion is soft, stirring after 2½ minutes. Stir in rice, pimentos, juice from clams (set clams aside), broth, and sausage slices. Cover and microwave on **HIGH (100%)** for 15 minutes or until rice has absorbed all liquid; give dish a half-turn after 7½ minutes.

Stir drained clams into rice mixture and lay chicken on top. Cover and microwave on **HIGH (100%)** for 3 minutes or until chicken is hot. Garnish with green onions and cilantro. Makes 6 servings.

Per serving: 449 calories, 45 g protein, 32 g carbohydrates, 14 g total fat, 122 mg cholesterol, 1,080 mg sodium

CHICKEN & SUMMER FRUIT SALAD

Preparation time: 15 to 20 minutes
Microwaving time: 6 to 8 minutes

- ⅓ cup slivered blanched almonds
  Chutney Dressing (facing page)
  Micro-steamed Chicken Breasts (at left), cut into bite-size chunks
- ½ cup pitted, halved sweet cherries
- 4 to 6 firm-ripe apricots, pitted and cut into bite-size slivers
- ¼ cup sliced green onions (including tops)
  Salt
- 1 large firm-ripe avocado
- 3 to 4 cups watercress sprigs, washed and crisped
  Orange wedges

Spread almonds in an 8- or 9-inch microwave-safe baking dish. Microwave, uncovered, on **HIGH (100%)**

for 6 to 8 minutes or until almonds are golden, stirring every 2 minutes. Set aside.

Prepare Chutney Dressing. In a large bowl, combine chicken, cherries, apricots, onions, and dressing. Season to taste with salt. (At this point, you may cover and refrigerate for up to 3 hours.)

Pit, peel, and slice avocado. Line 6 plates with watercress; mound chicken salad in center. Arrange avocado slices around salad. Garnish with almonds and orange wedges. Makes 6 servings.

Chutney Dressing. In a small bowl, stir together ⅓ cup *each* **mayonnaise** and **sour cream**; 2 tablespoons **Major Grey's chutney**, coarsely chopped; 1 teaspoon grated **orange peel**; and ⅛ teaspoon **ground nutmeg**.

Per serving: 436 calories, 38 g protein, 17 g carbohydrates, 25 g total fat, 98 mg cholesterol, 369 mg sodium

PASTA WITH CHICKEN & SAUSAGE

✳   ✳   ✳   ✳   ✳

Preparation time: About 15 minutes
Microwaving time: 20 to 21 minutes

- 1 **tablespoon butter or margarine**
- 1 **mild Italian sausage (about 3 oz.), casing removed, meat crumbled**
- 1 **small red bell pepper, seeded and cut into thin strips**
- 1 **teaspoon Italian herb seasoning or ¼ teaspoon *each* dry basil, dry oregano leaves, dry thyme leaves, and dry marjoram leaves**
- 1 **package (9 oz.) fresh linguine or fettuccine**
- 1 **can (14½ oz.) regular-strength chicken broth**
- ½ **cup *each* dry white wine and whipping cream**

Micro-steamed Chicken Breasts (facing page), cut into bite-size chunks
- ¼ **cup *each* minced parsley and freshly grated Parmesan cheese**
- **Salt and pepper**

Preheat a 2- to 2½-quart or 10-inch square microwave browning dish on **HIGH (100%)** for 4½ minutes. Using oven mitts, carefully remove dish to a heatproof surface. Add butter and swirl to melt; then add crumbled sausage and let brown for 3 minutes, turning after 1½ minutes.

Add bell pepper and Italian herb seasoning. Cover and microwave on **HIGH (100%)** for 3 minutes or until pepper is soft and sausage appears cooked, stirring after 1½ minutes. Spoon out mixture and set aside.

Lay pasta level in browning dish. Pour broth, wine, and cream over pasta. Cover and microwave on **HIGH (100%)** for 10 minutes, stirring every 3 minutes; pasta should be tender to bite.

Add chicken to pasta along with sausage-pepper mixture. Microwave, uncovered, on **HIGH (100%)** for 2 to 3 minutes or until chicken is hot. Add parsley and cheese; season to taste with salt and pepper. Mix with 2 forks to blend. Makes 6 servings.

Per serving: 450 calories, 45 g protein, 27 g carbohydrates, 17 g total fat, 177 mg cholesterol, 789 mg sodium

MU SHU CHICKEN

✳   ✳   ✳   ✳   ✳

Preparation time: About 15 minutes
Microwaving time: About 15 minutes

Micro-steamed Chicken Breasts and reserved marinade (facing page)
- 1 **tablespoon salad oil**
- 2 **teaspoons Oriental sesame oil**

- ½ **pound mushrooms, thinly sliced**
- 1 **medium-size onion, thinly slivered**
- 2 **cups shredded iceberg lettuce**
- 2 **large eggs, well beaten**
- 12 **flour tortillas (*each* about 8 inches in diameter)**
- **Hoisin sauce**
- **Sliced green onions (including tops)**
- **Fresh cilantro (coriander) leaves**

Cut chicken into bite-size strips. Set chicken and marinade aside.

Preheat a 2- to 2½-quart or 10-inch square microwave browning dish on **HIGH (100%)** for 4½ minutes. Using oven mitts, carefully remove dish to a heatproof surface.

Add salad oil and sesame oil to dish; swirl dish to coat bottom. Add mushrooms and slivered onion; wait until sizzling stops. Then microwave, uncovered, on **HIGH (100%)** for 6 minutes, stirring after 3 minutes. Onion should be soft; almost all liquid from mushrooms should have evaporated. Add chicken, lettuce, and ¼ cup of the marinade. Stir to blend. Cover and microwave on **HIGH (100%)** for about 2 minutes or until mixture is hot. Stir in eggs. Microwave, uncovered, on **HIGH (100%)** for 1 minute or just until eggs begin to set, stirring after 30 seconds. Cover and set aside.

To heat tortillas, enclose them in a plastic bag (or, if using a package of 12 tortillas, poke 3 or 4 holes in top of package). Microwave on **HIGH (100%)** for 1 to 1½ minutes or until hot through.

To eat, spoon chicken mixture into tortillas; add hoisin, green onions, and cilantro to taste. Makes 6 servings.

Per serving: 483 calories, 44 g protein, 55 g carbohydrates, 8 g total fat, 156 mg cholesterol, 883 mg sodium

HERBED CHICKEN WITH ARTICHOKES

Preparation time: 5 to 10 minutes
Microwaving time: 12 to 14 minutes
Standing time: 2 minutes

A savory mushroom-tomato sauce coats tender chicken breasts and artichoke hearts.

2 tablespoons butter or margarine
¼ pound mushrooms, thinly sliced
1 clove garlic, minced or pressed
1 can (8 oz.) tomato sauce
½ teaspoon *each* dry basil, dry oregano leaves, and ground turmeric
3 whole chicken breasts (about 1 lb. *each*), skinned, boned, and split
1 jar (6 oz.) marinated artichoke hearts, drained
Paprika
½ cup sour cream

Place butter in a 2- to 2½-quart microwave-safe baking dish. Microwave, uncovered, on **HIGH (100%)** for about 35 seconds or until butter is melted. Add mushrooms and garlic to dish; stir to coat with butter. Microwave, uncovered, on **HIGH (100%)** for 3 minutes, stirring after 1½ minutes. Stir in tomato sauce, basil, oregano, and turmeric.

Rinse chicken, pat dry, and place in sauce. Turn to coat; then arrange in a single layer, positioning thickest parts of breasts toward outside of dish. Cover and microwave on **HIGH (100%)** for 4 minutes. Turn chicken to bring uncooked portions to outside of dish; tuck artichokes between chicken pieces. Scoop sauce over chicken and artichokes.

Microwave, uncovered, on **HIGH (100%)** for 4 to 6 minutes, giving dish a half-turn every 2 minutes. Cover; let stand for 2 minutes. Chicken should no longer be pink in thickest part; cut to test.

To serve, sprinkle chicken with paprika; top each portion with sour cream. Makes 6 servings.

Per serving: 282 calories, 36 g protein, 7 g carbohydrates, 12 g total fat, 104 mg cholesterol, 521 mg sodium

---

Pictured on the cover

QUICK PAELLA

Preparation time: About 20 minutes
Microwaving time: About 39 minutes

Garnish this classic Spanish dish with chopped green onions and fresh cilantro leaves, if you like.

4 large chicken drumsticks (1¼ to 1½ lbs. *total*)
Salt, black pepper, and paprika
2 tablespoons olive oil or salad oil
¾ pound linguisa sausage or kielbasa (Polish sausage), cut into ¼-inch-thick slanting slices
2 cloves garlic, minced or pressed
1 large red bell pepper, seeded and chopped
⅛ teaspoon *each* ground saffron and ground red pepper (cayenne)
½ teaspoon *each* dry basil and dry oregano leaves
½ cup dry white wine
1½ cups regular-strength chicken broth
1¼ cups long-grain white rice
16 medium-large raw shrimp (about ½ lb. *total*), shelled (leave tails attached) and deveined

Rinse chicken and pat dry. Lightly sprinkle with salt, black pepper, and paprika; set aside.

Preheat a 2- to 2½-quart or 10-inch square microwave browning dish on **HIGH (100%)** for 4½ minutes. Using oven mitts, carefully remove dish to a heatproof surface. Add oil and swirl dish to coat bottom. Quickly add chicken, rounded side down, in a single layer. Wait until sizzling stops; then turn chicken over and arrange with thickest parts toward outside of dish. Cover and microwave on **HIGH (100%)** for 8 minutes, giving dish a half-turn after 4 minutes. Lift out chicken; set aside.

Add sausage, garlic, and bell pepper to dish; turn to coat with drippings. Cover and microwave on **HIGH (100%)** for 3 minutes. If desired, transfer sausage mixture and drippings to a shallow 2½- to 3-quart microwave-safe serving dish.

Add saffron, ground red pepper, basil, oregano, wine, broth, and rice to sausage mixture. Set chicken on top. Cover and microwave on **HIGH (100%)** for 20 minutes or until rice has absorbed all liquid, giving dish a half-turn after 10 minutes.

Push shrimp into rice. Cover; microwave on **HIGH (100%)** for 3 minutes or until shrimp turn pink. Makes 4 servings.

Per serving: 772 calories, 46 g protein, 51 g carbohydrates, 41 g total fat, 212 mg cholesterol, 1,447 mg sodium

*Slender baby carrots and a garnish of fresh herbs flank our
Florentine Turkey Rolls (recipe on page 89). For the prettiest presentation,
slice each roll to reveal its deep green spinach-cheese stuffing; then
spoon on the silky, nutmeg-seasoned mushroom sauce.*

CHEDDAR CHICKEN WITH CRACKED WHEAT

✻   ✻   ✻   ✻   ✻   ✻   ✻

Preparation time: About 30 minutes
Microwaving time: About 15 minutes

Microwave mushrooms and cracked wheat in a rosemary-seasoned broth, then mix in chunks of chicken and top the mixture with Cheddar cheese.

- 2 tablespoons butter or margarine
- ¼ pound mushrooms, thinly sliced
- 1 clove garlic, minced or pressed
- ½ cup cracked wheat (bulgur)
- 2 tablespoons instant minced onion
- ½ teaspoon dry rosemary
- ¼ teaspoon pepper
- 1¼ cups regular-strength chicken broth
- 3½ to 4 cups bite-size pieces cooked chicken (about a 4-lb. frying chicken; see page 77 for directions for cooking chicken)
- 1½ cups (6 oz.) shredded Cheddar cheese
  Paprika

Place butter in a shallow 2-quart microwave-safe baking dish. Microwave, uncovered, on **HIGH (100%)** for about 35 seconds or until butter is melted. Add mushrooms and garlic to dish; microwave, uncovered, on **HIGH (100%)** for 3 minutes. Stir in wheat, onion, rosemary, pepper, and broth. Cover and microwave on **HIGH (100%)** for 8 minutes or until wheat is tender and liquid has been absorbed.

Stir chicken into wheat mixture. Sprinkle cheese evenly over top, then lightly sprinkle with paprika. Microwave, uncovered, on **HIGH (100%)** for 3 minutes or until chicken is hot and cheese is melted. Makes 4 servings.

Per serving: 573 calories, 52 g protein, 21 g carbohydrates, 30 g total fat, 177 mg cholesterol, 746 mg sodium

CHICKEN LIVERS WITH BACON & ONION

✻   ✻   ✻   ✻   ✻   ✻   ✻

Preparation time: 10 to 15 minutes
Microwaving time: 15 minutes
Standing time: 3 minutes

Make sure the livers are still pink in the center when you remove them from the microwave, since they continue to cook while standing.

- 2 tablespoons all-purpose flour
- ¼ teaspoon *each* salt and pepper
- ¼ teaspoon dry rosemary
- ¾ pound chicken livers, cut in half and drained
- 4 slices bacon
- 1 small onion, thinly sliced and separated into rings
- 1 tablespoon Madeira or dry sherry
  Chopped parsley

On a rimmed plate, stir together flour, salt, pepper, and rosemary. Dredge chicken livers in flour mixture and set aside.

Place bacon in a 2- to 2½-quart or 10-inch square microwave browning dish. Cover with a paper towel and microwave on **HIGH (100%)** for 3 minutes or until slices look crisp (they'll become crisper on standing). Place bacon on another paper towel and let drain. Pour off and reserve all but 1 tablespoon of the drippings. Add onion to drippings remaining in dish; stir to coat. Microwave, uncovered, on **HIGH (100%)** for 5 minutes or until onion is soft, stirring after 2½ minutes. Remove from dish and set aside. Wipe dish clean.

Preheat empty browning dish on **HIGH (100%)** for 3 minutes. Using oven mitts, carefully remove dish to a heatproof surface. Add 1½ tablespoons of the reserved bacon drippings and tilt dish to coat bottom.

Immediately place chicken livers, sides not touching, in hot drippings. Slightly tilt dish so drippings touch each liver piece. Wait until sizzling stops; then turn livers over and bring any pieces that look raw to outside of dish. Sprinkle with Madeira. Cover and microwave on **HIGH (100%)** for 2 minutes. Bring any pieces that still look raw to outside of dish and push cooked ones to center; sprinkle onion over livers. Cover and microwave on **HIGH (100%)** for 2 minutes. All livers should be very pink in center; cut to test. Let stand, covered, for 3 minutes.

To serve, crumble bacon over livers and sprinkle with parsley. Makes 2 servings.

Per serving: 505 calories, 36 g protein, 14 g carbohydrates, 33 g total fat, 778 mg cholesterol, 717 mg sodium

Pictured on page 87
FLORENTINE TURKEY ROLLS

✳   ✳   ✳   ✳   ✳   ✳   ✳

Preparation time: About 15 minutes
Microwaving time: About 22 minutes

To make this elegant entrée for four, you wrap thin slices of turkey breast around a savory spinach and Swiss cheese filling, then swath the rolls in a creamy mushroom-wine sauce. You might serve buttered carrots and a mixed green salad alongside.

  1½   tablespoons butter or margarine
  ¼   pound mushrooms, thinly sliced
  1½   tablespoons all-purpose flour
  ⅛   teaspoon *each* ground nutmeg and
        ground white pepper
  ½   cup *each* regular-strength chicken broth,
        dry white wine, and half-and-half
  4   turkey breast steaks (about 5 oz. *each*),
        cut ½ inch thick
  1   package (10 oz.) frozen chopped spinach,
        thawed and squeezed dry
  1½   cups (6 oz.) shredded Swiss cheese

Place butter in a shallow 2- to 2½-quart microwave-safe baking dish. Microwave, uncovered, on **HIGH (100%)** for 30 to 35 seconds or until butter is melted. Add mushrooms; stir to coat with butter. Microwave, uncovered, on **HIGH (100%)** for 3 minutes, stirring once. Blend flour, nutmeg, and white pepper into mushroom mixture. Gradually stir in broth, wine, and half-and-half to make a smooth sauce. Microwave, uncovered, on **HIGH (100%)** for 6 minutes or until sauce boils and thickens, stirring every 2 minutes.

Rinse turkey steaks and pat dry, then place between 2 sheets of wax paper. Using a flat-surfaced mallet, pound each steak to a thickness of ¼ inch.

In a bowl, mix spinach, 1 cup of the cheese, and 3 tablespoons of the mushroom sauce. Place a fourth of the filling at one end of each turkey steak; roll to enclose. Place rolls, seam side down, in remaining sauce in baking dish; spoon some of the sauce up over tops of rolls.

Cover and microwave on **HIGH (100%)** for 5 minutes. Rearrange rolls, bringing those in center to ends of dish; cover and microwave on **HIGH (100%)** for 5 minutes. Sprinkle remaining ½ cup cheese over rolls. Microwave, uncovered, on **HIGH (100%)** for 2 minutes or until cheese is melted and turkey meat is no longer pink; cut to test.

To serve, place one roll on each of 4 dinner plates; cut each roll diagonally into ½-inch-thick slices. Arrange slices, overlapping slightly, to reveal spinach stuffing; spoon a fourth of the sauce over and around each serving. Makes 4 servings.

Per serving: 438 calories, 50 g protein, 10 g carbohydrates, 22 g total fat, 150 mg cholesterol, 440 mg sodium

RASPBERRY-GLAZED TURKEY TENDERLOINS

✳   ✳   ✳   ✳   ✳   ✳   ✳

Preparation time: About 5 minutes
Microwaving time: 6 to 7 minutes

Turkey tenderloins—the strips of meat lying along either side of the breastbone—make a lean, light microwave entrée. Here, we've sauced the tenderloins with a sweet-sour raspberry glaze.

  2   turkey breast tenderloins
        (about 6 oz. *each*)
  ¼   cup seedless raspberry jam
  3   tablespoons raspberry vinegar
  2   tablespoons Dijon mustard
  1   teaspoon grated orange peel
  ¼   teaspoon dry thyme leaves
        Salt

Rinse turkey and pat dry. In a shallow 1½- to 2-quart microwave-safe baking dish, stir together jam, vinegar, mustard, orange peel, and thyme until well blended. Add turkey; turn to coat well with sauce.

Cover and microwave on **HIGH (100%)** for 3 minutes. Brush tenderloins with sauce; then arrange with uncooked portions toward outside of dish. Microwave, uncovered, on **HIGH (100%)** for 3 to 4 minutes or until meat is no longer pink in thickest part; cut to test. Season to taste with salt. Makes 2 servings.

Per serving: 326 calories, 40 g protein, 32 g carbohydrates, 4 g total fat, 106 mg cholesterol, 569 mg sodium

A company dinner for four in under 40 minutes? Here it is—
Curried Game Hens with Papaya & Chutney (recipe on facing page). Serve the
browned hen halves and sweet papaya slices with fresh pineapple and a
simple pilaf; offer lime wedges to squeeze over meat and fruit.

CURRIED GAME HENS WITH PAPAYA & CHUTNEY

❋   ❋   ❋   ❋   ❋   ❋   ❋

Preparation time: 5 to 10 minutes
Microwaving time: 24 to 26 minutes

Succulent game hen halves are accompanied with thick slices of papaya, briefly microwaved in the same spicy lime-chutney glaze that coats the birds.

2	small Rock Cornish game hens (about 1¼ lbs. *each*), cut into halves
	Salt and black pepper
¼	cup butter or margarine, melted
2	teaspoons curry powder
⅛	teaspoon ground red pepper (cayenne)
3	tablespoons Major Grey's chutney, chopped
2	tablespoons lime juice
1	large papaya, peeled, seeded, and cut into ½-inch-thick slices
	Lime wedges

Rinse hen halves, pat dry, and sprinkle lightly with salt and black pepper. Mix butter, curry powder, and red pepper; brush over skin sides of hens.

Preheat a 2- to 2½-quart or 10-inch square microwave browning dish on **HIGH (100%)** for 4½ minutes. Using oven mitts, carefully remove dish to a heatproof surface. Quickly press game hen halves, skin side down, against hot surface of dish; wait until sizzling stops, then turn hens skin side up. Cover and microwave on **HIGH (100%)** for 10 minutes, giving dish a half-turn after 5 minutes.

Stir chutney and lime juice into drippings in dish; brush mixture over hens. Turn hens to bring uncooked portions to outside of dish. Microwave, uncovered, on **HIGH (100%)** for 8 to 10 minutes or until meat near thighbone is no longer pink (cut to test), giving dish a half-turn after 4 minutes.

Place hens on a warm platter. Add papaya to browning dish and turn to coat with drippings. Microwave, uncovered, on **HIGH (100%)** for 1½ minutes or until papaya is hot. Arrange papaya around hens. Offer lime wedges to squeeze over individual servings. Makes 4 servings.

Per serving: 531 calories, 35 g protein, 18 g carbohydrates, 35 g total fat, 146 mg cholesterol, 249 mg sodium

BRAISED GAME HENS IN CHIANTI

❋   ❋   ❋   ❋   ❋   ❋   ❋

Preparation time: 5 to 10 minutes
Microwaving time: 24 to 27 minutes

Serve polenta or boiled potatoes alongside these saucy little birds.

2	small Rock Cornish game hens (about 1¼ lbs. *each*), cut into halves
	Ground white pepper
2	slices pancetta or bacon (about 2 oz. *total*), coarsely chopped
1	clove garlic, minced or pressed
½	teaspoon dry marjoram leaves
1	tablespoon tomato paste
1¼	cups Chianti or other dry red wine
2	tablespoons butter or margarine, melted
1	tablespoon all-purpose flour
	Chopped parsley

Rinse hen halves, pat dry, and sprinkle lightly with white pepper. Place pancetta in a 2- to 2½-quart or 10-inch square microwave browning dish. Cover with a paper towel and microwave on **HIGH (100%)** for 2 minutes or until pancetta is lightly browned, stirring after 1 minute. Lift pancetta from dish and set aside.

Preheat browning dish on **HIGH (100%)** for 2 minutes. Brown hens as directed in recipe above; turn skin side up. Blend garlic, marjoram, tomato paste, and wine into drippings; spoon over hens. Cover; microwave on **HIGH (100%)** for 10 minutes, giving dish a half-turn after 5 minutes.

Turn hens to bring uncooked portions to outside of dish; baste with sauce. Cover and microwave on **HIGH (100%)** for 8 to 10 minutes or until meat near thighbone is no longer pink (cut to test), giving dish a half-turn after 4 minutes. Place hens on a warm platter and keep warm.

In a small bowl, blend butter and flour. Slowly stir in ¼ cup of the wine sauce; then stir back into remaining sauce in dish. Microwave, uncovered, on **HIGH (100%)** for 2 to 3 minutes or until sauce boils, stirring every 30 seconds. Pour sauce over hens; top with pancetta and parsley. Makes 4 servings.

Per serving: 502 calories, 36 g protein, 4 g carbohydrates, 37 g total fat, 140 mg cholesterol, 294 mg sodium

TIPS FOR SAVING TIME & EFFORT

In this book, we've focused on cooking meals from scratch in the microwave. Still, we know that sometimes you won't be microwaving the entire meal—or even the whole entrée. But even on those days, the microwave can offer plenty of help.

On these pages, we've gathered tips you'll find useful at every stage of meal preparation. The microwave can get dinner off to a faster start, simply by defrosting the meat; it can help you redo a meal, by reheating leftovers, or improve a meal, by toasting croutons or drying herbs for seasoning. And of course, it eases the preparation of all kinds of dishes—by softening dried fruit, melting chocolate, even clarifying broth.

We begin here with pointers for thawing and reheating foods, then go on to give hints for everything from softening cream cheese to warming tortillas. Let these tips show you just how versatile and convenient your microwave oven can be!

Defrosting. You can defrost on any power level, but **MEDIUM-LOW (30%)** does the best job of defrosting evenly, so foods won't start cooking on the outside before they're thawed on the inside. Many ovens have a setting labeled "defrost," equivalent to 30% power on newer models.

The key to successful defrosting in the microwave is *even heat distribution.* Remember the following points:

■ *Remove meat from its package,* place it on a microwave-safe plate or dish, and cover with heavy-duty plastic wrap. *Don't* try to thaw meat right in its store wrapping—the styrofoam trays often used for packaging may melt.

■ *Separate pieces* of meat or poultry as soon as possible to let the microwaves reach all sides. Leave plenty of space between pieces; place thicker portions toward the outside.

■ *Stir or break up ground meats* with a fork as soon as possible.

■ *Remove thawed portions* of meat or poultry as soon as possible so that all the microwave energy will be directed to the still-frozen parts.

■ *Defrost large pieces of food—a roast or a whole turkey, chicken, or large fish—in increments,* alternating short periods of microwaving with equal amounts of standing time. For example, microwave on **MEDIUM-LOW (30%)** for 5 minutes, then let stand for 5 minutes. Continue in this way until the food is thawed. This method allows the heat to reach the center of foods without risk of cooking the outside.

Reheating. If you have a microwave, yesterday's meal can be reheated to look and taste just as it did the first time you served it. What's more, you can reheat right in the storage container or on an individual plate.

■ *For refrigerated casserole-type leftovers,* start by storing leftovers in a microwave-safe container; cover with a lid or heavy-duty plastic wrap. To reheat, microwave on **HIGH (100%)** for 2 minutes per cup of refrigerated food; stir (if possible) or rotate the dish halfway through the heating time.

■ *For a plate of room-temperature food,* position dense or thick portions at the edges of the plate. Arrange lighter, more delicate foods such as leafy vegetables in the center. Cover and microwave on **HIGH (100%)** for 1 to 1½ minutes or until heated through.

Tricks with plastic wrap. Heavy-duty plastic wrap is a good "lid" for microwaved foods. Here are two tips you'll find helpful.

■ *To simplify the job of stirring food in a covered casserole,* cut a slit in the center of the plastic and insert a wooden spoon. That way, you won't need to remove or replace the plastic every time you stir. If the dish must stay tightly covered during cooking, remove the spoon after each stir and patch the slit with a small piece of plastic wrap.

■ *To allow for expansion during cooking,* you can pleat plastic wrap. Simply fold the plastic in 1½-inch pleats before covering the dish.

Softening cream cheese. Unwrap 1 small package (3 oz.) cream cheese and place it in a 10-ounce microwave-safe custard cup or bowl. Cover and microwave on **MEDIUM (50%)** for 30 seconds to 1 minute. For 1 large package (8 oz.) cream cheese, microwave for 1½ to 2 minutes.

Softening butter. Set ½ cup (¼ lb.) butter on a microwave-safe plate. Microwave butter, uncovered, on **MEDIUM-LOW (30%)** for 1 minute.

Melting butter. Place ½ cup (¼ lb.) butter in a 10-ounce microwave-safe custard cup or bowl. Microwave, uncovered, on **HIGH (100%)** for 1 minute.

Clarifying butter. The water and milk solids in butter tend to burn during cooking, so you may want to remove them before you use butter for sautéing. This process is called *clarifying,* and it's easily done in the microwave. Just cut ½ cup (¼ lb.) butter into 1-tablespoon pieces; place in a 2-cup glass measure. Microwave, uncovered, on **HIGH (100%)** for 2 minutes or until completely melted and bubbly. Skim and discard solids from top of liquid. Slowly pour clear liquid into another glass measure, leaving milky solids behind; discard solids. You should have ⅓ cup clarified butter.

Clarifying broth. Broths for aspics and consommés should be crystal-clear. Clarifying broth over direct heat on the range is a tedious task, but in the microwave it's simple.

Pour 4 cups broth into an 8-cup glass measure. Then separate 4 eggs; place whites in a small bowl, set shells aside, and reserve yolks for other uses. Beat whites until stiff; stir whites and shells into broth and let solids collect on surface. Then microwave, uncovered, on **HIGH (100%)** for 5 minutes or until broth begins to boil. Wet a clean dishtowel with warm water and wring dry. Place towel over a wire strainer set over a large bowl. Scoop egg whites and shells into towel, then slowly pour in hot broth. Broth that collects in bowl will be clarified.

Drying herbs. Fresh herbs dried in the microwave have superior fragrance and color. Scatter 2 cups loosely packed washed and dried fresh herb leaves or sprigs evenly on a double thickness of paper towels. Microwave, uncovered, on **HIGH (100%)** for 4 minutes or until herbs look dry. Store tightly covered.

Shelling nuts. To shell nuts such as pecans or walnuts easily, place 2 cups nuts in the shell and 1 cup water in a 9-inch microwave-safe baking dish. Cover and microwave on **HIGH (100%)** for 1½ minutes. Drain, then shell.

Blanching nuts. To blanch ½ pound (about 1⅓ cups) shelled nuts, place in a single layer in a 9-inch

microwave-safe baking dish; add ¼ cup hot water. Cover; microwave on **HIGH (100%)** for 3 minutes. Drain. Turn nuts onto a clean dishtowel; use towel to rub off skins.

Toasting nuts. To toast ½ cup pine nuts or whole or slivered blanched almonds, arrange nuts in a single layer in a 9- or 10-inch microwave-safe baking dish. Microwave, uncovered, on **HIGH (100%)** for 6 to 8 minutes, stirring every 2 minutes. Nuts should be just golden; they'll continue to cook while standing.

Making croutons. Place ¼ cup butter or margarine in a 7- by 11-inch microwave-safe baking dish. Microwave, uncovered, on **HIGH (100%)** for about 45 seconds or until melted. Stir in about 4 cups fresh bread cubes and 1 teaspoon dry herbs (optional). Microwave, uncovered, on **HIGH (100%)** for 4 to 6 minutes, stirring every minute. Then let croutons stand for 5 minutes to dry completely.

Scalding milk. To heat milk to scalding for soups, sauces, or custards, pour 1 cup milk into a 4-cup glass measure. Cover and microwave on **HIGH (100%)** for 1½ minutes or until milk registers 180° to 185°F on a thermometer (remove milk from oven to test).

Melting chocolate. Unwrap 1 square (1 oz.) unsweetened or semisweet chocolate and place in a small microwave-safe bowl or dish. Cover and microwave on **MEDIUM (50%)** for 2 minutes or until soft but not completely melted (chocolate will scorch if overheated). Stir until fully melted.

Soaking mushrooms. If you need to soak dried morels, porcini, or shiitake mushrooms for a recipe, here's a way to do the job quickly.

■ *For morels,* place 2 tablespoons (1 oz.) dried morels and ¼ cup water in a 2-cup glass measure. Cover and microwave on **HIGH (100%)** for 3 minutes or until soft.

■ *For porcini (cèpes) or whole shiitake mushrooms,* discard mushroom stems; rinse caps in cold water to remove grit. Arrange 8 large mushroom caps, bottom sides up, in a single layer on a microwave-safe plate. Sprinkle with 1 tablespoon water. Cover and microwave on **HIGH (100%)** for 4 minutes or just until soft.

Softening hard dried fruit. Dried fruit that has become too hard is easy to soften in the microwave. Place dried fruit in a pie plate (arrange apricots, apples, peaches, and pears cavity side up). Sprinkle lightly with water. Cover tightly; microwave on **HIGH (100%)** for 15 to 30 seconds or just until soft.

Softening brown sugar. Break up about 1 cup brown sugar; spread in a microwave-safe pie plate or dish. Set a ½-inch-thick wedge of apple on top of sugar. Cover and microwave on **HIGH (100%)** for 30 to 45 seconds or until sugar is soft.

Decrystallizing honey or jam. If honey or jam container has a metal lid, remove lid. Then place container in microwave; microwave, uncovered, on **HIGH (100%)** for 1 to 1½ minutes per cup of honey or jam or until sugar crystals have melted.

Warming tortillas. To soften an unopened package of 10 to 12 flour or corn tortillas (*each 6 to 8 inches in diameter*), poke 3 or 4 holes in the package and place it on the oven floor. Microwave on **HIGH (100%)** for 1 to 1½ minutes. To heat just a few tortillas, wrap them in paper towels and microwave on **HIGH (100%)** for 6 to 7 seconds per tortilla.

Index

*Quick and colorful, light yet satisfying—Hot Chicken Salad in
Tomato Cups (recipe on page 45) is a guaranteed suppertime success.
Red, ripe tomatoes hold a chunky chicken-artichoke filling enlivened
with pimento strips, green onions, and Cheddar cheese.*